Blueprint for Romance

Blueprint for Romance

Shannon M. Harris

SAPPHIRE BOOKS

SALINAS, CALIFORNIA

Blueprint for Romance
Copyright © 2019 by Shannon M. Harris. All rights reserved.

ISBN - 978-1-948232-71-5

This is a work of fiction - names, characters, places, and incidents are the product of the author's imagination or are used fictitiously. Any resemblance to actual persons living or dead, business, events or locales is entirely coincidental.

All rights reserved. No part of this publication may be reproduced, distributed, or transmitted in any form or by any means, including photocopying, recording, or other electronic or mechanical methods, without written permission of the publisher.

Editor - Kaycee Hawn
Book Design - LJ Reynolds
Cover Design - Fineline Cover Design

Sapphire Books Publishing, LLC
P.O. Box 8142
Salinas, CA 93912
www.sapphirebooks.com

Printed in the United States of America
First Edition – September 2019

This and other Sapphire Books titles can be found at
www.sapphirebooks.com

Dedication

This one is dedicated to all the hours I spent pouring over this story. It was a long but worthwhile process.

Acknowledgments

Thank you to Chris and everyone at Sapphire books for all that they do. A shout out to Linda who helped me get this story into shape, and to all the readers who chose this book to pick up.

Chapter One

Dylan Lake pushed a hand through her tangled blond curls as she observed herself in the bathroom mirror. Fatigue danced around her brown eyes and a spattering of freckles stood out across her nose. Disgusted at the image reflected, she dipped both hands in the sink and splashed cold water on her face. It was days like these she felt older than her thirty-five years.

Emma, her seven-year-old daughter, didn't always have bad nights, but when they hit, it left them both drained and exhausted. Emma had woken her up around two a.m. and hadn't fallen asleep until six. Now at nine o'clock, Dylan felt the brief five hours of sleep she'd gotten.

When Emma was two years old, she and her dad were in a car accident that left Ian dead and Emma pinned against the side of the car. Because Emma sustained so much damage, the doctors amputated her right leg above the knee. Losing first her husband, then learning Emma's life had hung in the balance were the most excruciating experiences of Dylan's life. The healing process had taken years, but Dylan and Emma had made it through and now both were on the right path.

A happy child, Emma loved to draw and paint, along with coming up with new creations for her numerous dollhouses. Her collection of miniature items took up half of her room, but Dylan wouldn't have it any other way. Seeing the joy on Emma's face was well worth the pain of occasionally stepping on one of the miniature pieces. Lately, Emma had taken to buying Lego figures and decorating her dollhouses with them. Money was tight, but Dylan did her best to make sure Emma had most of the things she wanted.

After Ian's death, it became hard, especially finding out he had quit the payments on their health insurance a few months prior to the accident. Five days into Emma's hospital stay, she was moved to a children's hospital where her medical bills would be paid, but that still left the bill for five days prior for Dylan to cover. It had come as a shock when she received the bill for almost a hundred and fifty thousand dollars.

She could have let the bills go into a collection agency but that wasn't how she was raised, so the fifty thousand received from Ian's life insurance and the ten thousand from the sale of their house went directly to pay for Emma's bills. Monthly payments were arranged for the remaining amount. Despite his tight budget, her dad had contributed a hundred dollars a month to help pay it off and for that, she would always be grateful. But she wasn't sure how much longer she could do it. Bankruptcy held an option, but she wasn't ready to throw in the towel, no matter how many work hours were required to pay off the balance.

Six months after Ian was buried, Dylan and Emma moved in with her mom to make ends meet. A selling point had also been that Emma's rehabilitation center was only forty minutes away from her mom's house. It became a turning point in her life when realizing at thirty-one she couldn't do it on her own. It was a hard pill to swallow but she would do anything for her daughter, including moving in with her mom.

Emma was happy, and Dylan enjoyed getting the chance to know her mom all over again, even if money was tight. She was proud but, like anyone struggling to pay their bills and put food on the table, she'd broken down and signed up for assistance. It didn't bother her as much as it used to when someone would make a snide comment when she would use her food card to buy ice cream sandwiches for her daughter as a snack. Emma went to hell and back and Dylan didn't care what a stranger thought of her. Until someone walked in her shoes, they could keep their pointless opinions to themselves.

Ian's death happened five years ago, but sometimes a memory would hit of that tragic time, making it seem almost like yesterday, and she'd be stuck replaying moments in their life together. From joy to pain, then all over again. It was a process she was still learning to deal with. Even though she had dealt with his death and was ready to move on, it would always feel like a tiny part of her was missing. Especially while in bed at night when she would reach for him, only to feel an empty space beside her. She didn't wish, even for her worst enemy, to lose their spouse. The pain was piercing.

At times, remembering the notification from the police officer of the accident would slam into her and she'd break down all over again. There were moments she cursed Ian for letting the insurance go, but he had provided for them and had loved her and Emma. She would never get the chance to ask him why but knew he would have never wanted her to struggle. He loved them, but at times it all seemed for naught. She had trusted him to provide health insurance, but in the end, even if he hadn't meant it, her trust in him fractured. Thank God, he'd kept his life insurance up to date.

They had known each other in high school, but lost touch while they were both in college on opposite sides of the country. After Dylan graduated, she had met up with Ian again in their home town and rekindled their relationship. It had felt natural from there to get married and have a child.

She'd dated off and on during college but no one she wanted to make a life with. There was one woman, but that ended abruptly when she opted to intern overseas. After coming out as bisexual in high school, her parents never treated her any differently and she would always be grateful for their open acceptance of her.

After Ian died, it felt like her life had slowed to a crawl, especially while spending so much time in the hospital with Emma. The doctors had given her a fifty percent chance of making it and although Dylan wasn't religious, she had prayed to every deity she could think of to save her baby's life. During that time, the weight gain came. She didn't necessarily hate her body, but on some days, she wished to lose the extra weight. Going from a size six to twelve proved eye opening and as much as she tried to discipline her eating habits, the extra pounds stayed. It had taken a lot of time for her to accept herself, but it was a wonderful place to be.

Dylan applied the final touches of make-up and fixed her hair. Her reflection in the mirror looked like she hadn't slept, but, at least now, she looked presentable. With a final look in the mirror, satisfied with what she saw, she joined her mom in the kitchen.

"Good morning, sweetheart." Iris Dunmore was a formidable woman at sixty-three, and Dylan's rock.

Looking at her now, Dylan swallowed the lump in her throat. If it hadn't been for her mom, she didn't know if she would have survived. Those first few months after Ian's death were the hardest of her life. And if it hadn't been for Emma, Dylan wasn't sure what her outcome would have been. For the first year after Ian's death, Dylan kept a bottle of pain killers, that were Ian's from knee surgery, in the drawer by the bed, but with the help of her mother and a therapist, she was able to work through her grief in a healthy way. Never would she have left her daughter, but it scared her that death was an option once considered.

"Sweetheart, I know that look." Iris waved her hand in the air. "Stop before you ruin your make-up. Sit. I'll get you a cup of coffee."

Dylan bypassed her mom's outstretched arm and pulled her into a hug. "I love you, Mom."

"I love you too." Iris patted her back. Once Dylan sat with a cup of coffee, Iris went on. "How's Emma this morning?"

"Asleep. Finally." Dylan took a sip of her coffee, closing her eyes as the caramel tones danced on her tongue. "It was a long night."

"By the time I'd gotten out of bed when she screamed, you were already with her. What was it this time?"

"Another nightmare."

"Should we up her sessions with Dr. Kline?"

"No. Dr. Kline said the nightmares would come and go. She already sees her once every two weeks." Dylan hated that her baby still suffered from the accident. On bad nights, Emma would wake up screaming and when realizing her right leg was gone, she would have a panic attack. Dylan wished she could take her child's pain away. She would give anything in the world for that to happen, but knew it was a wasted wish. If sitting up with Emma half the night was what she had to do, the lack of sleep was a small price to pay for Emma's pain and peace of mind.

Iris nodded and placed a bowl of fruit salad, granola, and yogurt on the table. "Are you still going to be able to help your cousin at her restaurant today?"

With her spoon halfway to her mouth, Dylan groaned. "Yes, we can use the extra money." She popped the spoon in her mouth and hummed as the spice of the granola danced on her tongue. Working on her day off wasn't ideal, but the money, along with the tips, would be worth it.

"You could always use extra money in the bank." Iris took the seat across from her.

"I know." Macy, older than Dylan by three years, owned the Burger Café, a restaurant in the next town over. Not that Dylan didn't want to help, but it was difficult to get the smell of grease out of her clothes after a workday at the restaurant. When she'd first moved to town, she'd readily taken the job Macy had offered, but soon realized it wasn't for her. "She said eleven, right?"

"She did." Iris patted her hand then took a sip of coffee and sighed. "Emma and I will be fine. She plans to work on a new drawing anyway."

Dylan nodded. "It's all she talked about yesterday."

"It was." Iris held her coffee cup between her hands.

"All right." Dylan stood, stretched, then deposited her empty cup and bowl in the sink. "I'll see you later."

Dylan worked five days a week at The Town Square, a local hotel, in downtown Garriety as a housekeeper. It wasn't much but, as of right now, it at least paid the bills, and, most days, it afforded her the time to be there when Emma got home from school. She'd also gained a friend in her co-worker, Haley. They'd quickly hit it off after Dylan was hired and they tried to get together at least a couple of times a month outside of work. Dylan's dream was to become a florist one day and run her own shop, but as of right now, that's all it was, a dream. She didn't have the extra time to spend on silly notions with bills to pay and a disabled child to take care of.

The previous week, Dylan had gotten a quarter raise and her hours had changed. From now on she'd work Sunday to Wednesday and Friday. She felt grateful for the change in schedule that would allow her to accompany Emma to her Saturday activities. It would also allow her to find a job that she could work on Thursdays. She wasn't sure what jobs were available that would let her work only one day a week, but surely, something existed out there.

Haley had also been a catalyst in enrolling Emma in public school. Dylan had worried herself to death when she had investigated private schools for Emma. The cost had almost given her a heart attack. But Haley had even gone as far as creating a Power-Point presentation for enrolling in public school. Dylan was skeptical because of Emma's disability, but Emma's excitement over the tour of the school combined with Haley's presentation and the knowledgeable staff sealed the deal for Dylan. Though Emma had never had a panic attack while attending, Dylan made sure everyone was aware of her issues and the faculty had assured her that Emma's well-being was their number one priority. Emma had taken to it and quickly made a few friends. Dylan wanted Emma to live the fullest life she could. The panic attacks lessoned over the years, but Dylan knew from experience they could be debilitating.

Dylan leaned against her daughter's door and watched the rise and fall of her small chest, a well-loved penguin plush that her dad had given her for her first birthday held tightly in the right hand. The same penguin that Dylan had to perform emergency surgery on more than once over the years. Emma didn't feel sorry for herself, and Dylan wouldn't either. Emma was the strongest person she knew and took every opportunity to do something fun.

Emma was hooked on horseback riding, and they had an appointment for a riding lesson once every two weeks. If it wasn't for one of the local charities and the donations they received, Emma wouldn't have been able to take these classes. Dylan was grateful for everything she and Emma had received since the accident.

The forearm crutches Emma used from time to time were propped against the wall by her bed for easy access. Her wheelchair sat folded up in the corner of her room. Thankfully, with the help of some amazing organizations, Emma received a couple of prosthetic devices. One for everyday use and the other a running prosthetic that Emma wore when she played soccer. It became a life saver for them both to realize that Emma, with the help of technology, could participate with the other children in after school activities. Every few years, the prosthetic devices needed to be upgraded, but Dylan couldn't worry about that now. When the time came, she'd have all her paperwork in order and prayed that Emma would be allowed the prosthetics she would need.

Dylan had been diligent in teaching Emma how to care for her prosthetic limb. It could be a slow and tedious process, but they were both so thankful for the chance for Emma to live a normal life that they would go through the process together most days. Emma was still too young to take on the task herself, but when they had the extra time, Emma would take over the duty of caring for and washing her prosthetic socks and gel liners.

"You need to go," Iris said.

"I know." Dylan wiped a tear away.

Iris kissed her on the cheek. "Drawing this morning, then the Garriety Science Center later."

"Okay." Dylan hated for her mom to pay for Emma's way, but was also grateful. Her pride only stung a little every time Iris paid for something that Dylan should be paying for. Iris had told her more than once that they were in this together and after five years living under the same roof, Dylan started to believe it.

With a final look, Dylan turned and walked away. She hoped when Emma got older, she didn't resent the hand dealt her. Dylan would do what became necessary to ensure that didn't happen. No matter the sacrifices she'd had to make over the years. Even if that included dating.

Iris had told her countless times she needed to date more. That it wasn't good for Emma to be her entire life. Losing Ian had broken her heart, and even though it had healed over time, it still hurt. She'd dated over the years, but no one note-worthy, and no one she wanted to introduce to her daughter. There was one guy, but when he realized he wasn't the center of Dylan's world, it quickly fell apart. There weren't many people that wanted to deal with a handicapped child.

Dylan knew she'd get the same talk from her dad about dating when she saw him the following week when he took Emma fishing. When a teenager, Dylan's parents divorced, but her dad had always been there for them. Dylan knew if she ever needed anything, he'd be there at a moment's notice.

She'd yet to meet someone she would be willing to give her heart to. They'd have to be someone special, and at this point in her life, she wouldn't settle for less than she deserved. They would have to understand that Emma was her life and they would always come in second. She'd learned the hard way life was too short, and she didn't have time for games. No. She shook her head and backed her car out of the driveway. Love wasn't in her game plans. At least, not any time soon.

Chapter Two

Kat Anderson hummed as her two employees, Kyle and Reeva, put the finishing touches on their latest tiny house build. It truly was a labor of love over the last six months to get everything for the business planned and implemented, but the result standing proud in front of her felt good. With one final walk around, she joined the other two off to the side of the house.

Kyle had come to her from Washington State. His car carried all his possessions the first time he interviewed for the job. She had a sneaking suspicion he had also been sleeping in his car. Briley, her sister, wasn't sure about hiring him and voiced concerns, but Kat saw something in him. That, coupled with his previous job as a construction worker, and the positive recommendation from his former boss, sealed the deal for her. What sealed the deal for Kyle was the stipulation that he could live in the bunkhouse as part of his salary. They'd gotten along since day one and he turned out to be an excellent craftsman. When he showed interest in building custom cabinets, Kat knew he was going to be an excellent addition to her team.

On the other hand, Reeva was a harder sale. Brandon, Briley's business partner in their house flipping enterprise, had recommended Reeva after she was laid off from her job unexpectedly. Although she had worked in construction all her life and had a certification in plumbing, she also had a permanent chip on her shoulder. The first time Briley had met Reeva, Briley had brought her girlfriend Leah with her. Normally, Briley was chill, but Kat had to calm her down when Reeva made an inappropriate comment about how hot Leah was. Kat had fired her on the spot, but a few days later, Reeva, with a different attitude, came back and apologized to all of them. Kat wasn't one to hold a grudge and made it clear she wouldn't stand for that kind of behavior toward anyone. She hadn't had any trouble out of her since.

Where Reeva was tall and skinny, Kyle was short and stocky. They'd clashed a few times when they first started working together, but after the first few weeks both seemed to mellow out. Kat never asked what brought about the change and they didn't offer an explanation. If they stayed decent to each other and it didn't interfere with business, she wouldn't get involved in their squabble.

"Looks good, boss," Kyle said, rubbing his beard.

"The buyer should be pleased," Reeva added. From the moment Kat had met Reeva, she'd appreciated her short, almost buzz cut red hair. It wasn't just anyone who could pull the look off, but Reeva did it effortlessly. Her dimples didn't hurt either.

Five months ago, Kat had made an appointment to get her hair trimmed, but once at the salon, her eyes had zeroed in on a picture hanging on the wall and she'd decided to go for it. For years, she'd had a bob cut, but now her chestnut hair was short on the sides and longer on top. At least, long enough to spike it up if so desired. She wasn't sure she could pull the look off, but the stylist had promised it would work. Briley had given her hair the once over, high-fived her, and said how good it looked. The first few weeks, it took some getting used to but now, she loved it and kept on top of her hair appointments to keep it that way.

"He should be," Kat said. They'd hit a few snags with their first tiny house build but Kat had expected that. It was Kyle and Reeva's first time working in such a tiny medium, and Kat's first time with any type of construction. With Briley and Brandon's help, they had quickly found solutions to all their issues.

On more than one occasion, Briley and Kat had stayed up all night trying to figure out the answer to a problem. She'd spent more money on flowers for Leah over the last six months, as an apology for taking up so much of Briley's time, than she had on all her previous girlfriends combined. That might have been why they were all exes.

A year ago, when Kat decided to quit her accounting job, where she was set to make partner, to move to Garriety, her mom verbalized her displeasure. Briley, however, had stuck by her like glue. Even though two years older than Briley, her sister had always been her rock. They'd talked for hours over the three months Kat spent deciding what she wanted to do with the rest of her life. Briley's encouragement and straight forward voice of reason allowed Kat to take a chance on herself and future.

Her musings stopped when Kyle slapped her on the back. "How about the three of us go out for drinks to celebrate the completed house?"

"I'm game." Reeva rocked back on her heels and eyed Kat as if challenging her. Kat wasn't much of a drinker, and had no intention of getting wasted. The last time they'd gone drinking, Reeva and Kyle had made a contest out of who could drink the most. It was something to watch. Reeva and Kyle were so focused on beating each other, they didn't notice that Kat limited herself to a couple of beers. Kyle had lost, and showed up the next morning looking like death warmed over but managed to complete his assigned job.

"Can't. I'm watching my niece tonight." Briley and Leah were going on almost a year of dating and it was only a matter of time before they got engaged, considering Kat had gone ring shopping with Briley the previous week and Briley couldn't keep a secret to save her life.

Some days, she wished for what Briley and Leah shared. Their love was evident to anyone who spent any amount of time with them. Yes, she wanted what they had, but knew what they put into their relationship, and wasn't sure she had it in her to compromise so much. At least not right now. In the future, when more settled, and the business brought in a steady enough income that she could quit her part-time accounting job, she would go about finding someone to share her life. Maybe. Though it was not at the top of her long priority list.

Right now, they already had two more tiny house builds on the docket and she was meeting with two more people next week to discuss their options. The career demanded more than she'd expected, but she loved it and couldn't wait for it to become full time. Being able to create a home for someone was exhilarating and a high she didn't know she needed.

"You two have fun, though." Kat took one more look at the tiny house, then bid them a good evening. After six months of working closely together, they'd earned her trust and she now allowed Kyle to lock up the building and make sure everything was secure. He was becoming a friend, while Reeva stayed at arm's length. But Kat couldn't complain about her since she had a stellar work ethic and that's what mattered.

As Kat slid into the seat of her work truck, she searched her mind for where to take Griffin for dinner, recalling a recommendation from Kyle. It was always a new and exciting experience to spend time with her and she couldn't wait to see what the two of them could get into next.

Thirty minutes later, she pulled into her driveway and made her way inside the house for a quick shower. There were still a few things she wanted to do to make the space hers, like finishing the basement, but she had to admit it felt like home. She'd never felt like that when living in her condo. Maybe all she had needed to feel secure in her life was to set down roots.

As she passed by the large poster of Harley Quinn leading to the office, she saluted her, then walked into the office and greeted her ferret, Stripes. She had fallen in love with him the first time she'd laid eyes on him. His light red-brown guard hair was paired with a white undercoat, brown eyes, and a pink nose. She picked him up and lifted her phone to snap a picture for their Instagram page. She had to admit they made a fine pair. Once an adequate amount of cuddling had occurred, she made her way to the bedroom and scrounged through the closet as Stripes sat on the bed, staring at her. She made herself presentable in a pair of skinny jeans, a gray Anderson Tiny Homes t-shirt, to rep her brand, and a pair of white sneakers, then kissed Stripes on the head and bounded across the street to Briley and Leah's house. Before she could even knock on the door, it suddenly swung open, and a nervous Briley stepped out, shutting the door behind her, then pushed Kat back down the steps.

For the first time in a long time, Briley looked nervous. Good grief, she'd talked to her a few hours ago and she seemed all right. "What's wrong?"

Briley gnawed on her bottom lip and lifted a hand to run it through her hair, forgetting for a moment she had put it up in a bun, leaving it sticking out in some places, making her look like a wild animal. Kat held back her snicker because Briley was wired.

Briley stuffed her hands in the pocket of her sweatpants that had honestly seen better days. One leg had a split up the calf and holes littered the other leg. A baseball sized stain of unknown substance covered one knee. The red and yellow flip flops and pink tank-top depicting a unicorn added to the overall picture. Kat thought about taking a picture but figured now wasn't the time for blackmail material. Not with Briley looking so distressed.

"I'm going to do it." Briley balled her hands into fists.

"It?" Kat knew exactly what Briley meant, but it didn't hurt to egg her on.

"Don't be a smartass. Tonight. I'm doing it tonight." She nodded her head as if to convince herself and not Kat.

Instead of saying anything, she drew Briley into a hug and noticed over Briley's shoulder the front room curtain being pulled back and Leah watching them. "I'm proud of you and you don't have anything to be worried about. Well, at least not much to worry about. If I were you, I would change clothes before I asked the love of my life to marry me. Are you sure this," she said, pointing to Briley's clothes, "is the look you want to go with?"

Briley squeezed her tight, then pulled away. "I plan on it. A nice dinner out, then maybe a walk down by the river, then back here for dessert. I have everything planned. I've got this." She pointed to her own chest and Kat noticed the fingers of Briley's other hand squeezing something in her pocket. Briley carried that ring with her everywhere she went once she bought it. She was surprised Briley hadn't broken down and asked Leah before now or lost it. Her excitement was palpable. Kat had balked at the price of the ring, but Briley had barely blinked at it. One look at the ring and Briley had declared it perfect. Once Briley set her mind to something, she went for it. She'd announced that her bank account was healthy and wanted nothing more than to put a nice ring on Leah's finger. In the end, Kat admitted the ring was beautiful and looked like it was made for Leah.

"Yes, you do. Don't overthink this, Bri. She loves you. Now," she slipped her arm around Briley's shoulders, "I'm going to collect Griffin and you need to start working on your evening." At the front door, Kat turned Briley to face her, then squeezed her shoulders. "Relax. You've got the girl. There is no way Leah will say no."

"Say no to what?"

Kat flinched at the unexpected voice. They were both so lost in their own world, they didn't hear the front door open. Briley's eyes widened, and Kat tightened her grip on Briley's shoulders before they both turned to Leah, who stood in the open door. It would have been comical if it wasn't so serious.

Leah narrowed her eyes at them. "What are you two up to? Does it have anything to do with Briley being fidgety all week?" Leah was a force when she set her mind to something and one would never be able to tell she only stood five-foot-two, a good nine inches shorter than Kat, but the way she commanded a room made her seem larger than life. It was one of the things Kat appreciated, respected, and loved about her, but not at this moment.

"What?" Briley said, and Kat could see the sweat gather on her forehead. "Kat was being weird." She adjusted her glasses and Kat fought the urge not to roll her eyes. Leave it to Briley to make the situation even more forced.

"I know you two well enough. I don't buy it. What will I not say no to?" Leah looked from one to the other. "Does this have anything to do with those Christmas blueprints for the house I found stashed behind the cereal boxes in the kitchen cabinet? We can go back to pretending I never found them if you want to."

Kat was about to make up some bullshit story when Briley did the one thing she hadn't expected and dropped to one knee while taking the small black box out of her pocket. Kat didn't realize Briley had it in her, but quickly pulled out her phone and started recording, proud her little sister worked up the courage to do this. Although, a bit horrified that Briley decided to do this looking like a homeless person on a three-day bend.

"To marrying me." Briley opened the ring case and Leah covered her mouth and gasped. "Leah, I love you more than life itself. Will you do me the honor of becoming my wife?"

Kat took a step back when Leah squealed and pulled a grinning Briley up, allowing her to slip the ring on her finger. Briley picked Leah up and swung her around while they both cried, Leah's blond curls bouncing around them.

"Yes. A thousand times yes." Leah peppered kisses all over Briley's face.

"Say it again," Briley said.

"Yes."

Kat wasn't one to get emotional but seeing them both so happy warmed her heart. She was happy for them and glad she could be witness to their engagement, but at the same time, understood now more than ever what she was missing out on. Her choice to wait before finding her own Leah wasn't looking all that great at the moment. She'd come back to her senses, but now felt a tiny pull of loneliness in the pit of her stomach.

When they broke apart, Kat sent the video to both their phones, then grabbed them into a group hug. She kissed first Briley's, then Leah's cheek. "I'm so happy for you both."

"Thank you, Kat," Leah said, wiping her eyes. "I'm glad you recorded it."

Briley took her glasses off and wiped her eyes as well. "I had everything planned. Kat and I just talked about it." She looked disgusted with herself, but Kat had learned over the past year that Briley was putty in Leah's hands and didn't have any self-control around her.

Leah cupped her cheek. "My love, I couldn't imagine a more wonderful proposal."

"Really, Tiny?" Briley used the nickname she had for Leah, and grinned.

"Yes."

"Enough of that," Kat said, ushering them both inside. "No need to give the neighbors even more of a show. You know if they catch a tiny whiff of something, it's spread around town in seconds." Kat had learned over the last year and a half that, although it was a good neighborhood to live in, nothing stayed quiet for long. "I'm going to grab your daughter, then we're going to get out of your hair." Kat gave her sister a teasing smile. "Briley, you can still give her an evening she won't forget."

She didn't stick around, instead giving them their privacy, and walked down the hallway to Griffin's room where the child busily stuffed things into a Big Bird duffel bag she'd gotten for Christmas.

"Ready, monkey?" Kat stayed back by the door, awaiting Griffin's instructions.

A bob of the small head was her answer. Griffin was quickly expanding her vocabulary, but only talked when in the mood. Kat respected that.

"Let me help you." Griffin accepted the help then ran into the living room for goodbye kisses from her moms. With the duffle bag on one arm and Griffin on the other, Kat walked across the street to her house. Once Griffin's things were put in the living room, and she'd greeted Stripes, they were ready to go.

"Burgers for dinner?"

"Fries?"

"You bet, monkey." Kat ran after her once they were in the front yard and pretended to be a tickle monster.

Griffin still giggled when Kat buckled her into her car seat.

"I know of a place we can go." She'd never been before but Kyle swore by their burgers, proclaiming them the best he'd ever had. She would withhold judgement until she tried one, but being the best was a bit of a stretch considering Briley, the restaurant aficionado of the family, hadn't even heard of the restaurant before.

Double checking in the rearview mirror that Griffin was comfortable, Kat put the truck in reverse and backed out of the driveway. The burgers better be worth it because it was a forty-minute drive from her house and Griffin was not one for patience. She flipped the radio on, singing along with Griffin, as they made their way to the Burger Café.

Chapter Three

The Burger Café, a converted old gas station, looked a lot smaller than Kat expected from Kyle's description. The large sign that hung above the building almost dwarfed the restaurant itself and lit up the entire parking lot.

Cars filled almost every available parking space. It took Kat driving four times around the building until she noticed a car back out of a space. She sped up and pulled her truck in the vacated space. She hoped Kyle wasn't messing with her when he suggested this place because her patience was already wearing thin from finding a parking spot alone.

"We're here, monkey." From the frown on Griffin's face, her patience was also thinning.

Griffin grabbed the seatbelt. "I'm hungry."

"Me too." Kat hadn't had anything since lunchtime and her stomach had shown its displeasure on their drive here.

The straps of Griffin's backpack leash slid easily onto her shoulders and she walked a step in front of Kat as they made their way to the front door. The backpack allowed Griffin to have her hands free, and her parents the peace of mind that she was safe.

Kat held the door for an older couple walking out, and as soon as she caught the crowded space, she picked Griffin up, not wanting her to get trampled. The smell of the burgers intoxicated, and she held back a moan. The smell alone, she decided, would make this trip worth it.

The chatter around them and the workers behind the counter, along with the vintage photos on the wall, instantly put her at ease. Unlike Briley, Kat had always enjoyed being amid a crowd. It made her feel alive, like she was a part of something bigger.

After walking in, Kat stood off to the side to take in the space. A long counter ran along the far wall, and the grills and deep fryers were set right behind them in full view. Tables took up most of the available floor space. At first glance, they all looked to be filled, except for a few stools along the counter.

A large menu hung above the counter proclaiming build your own burger, up to ten patties, and a dozen different toppings to choose from, but only three sides; French fries, onion rings, or tater tots. It looked straight forward, and she wondered where to order, because it seemed like people were shouting out orders to the two cooks behind the counter. She stopped a man that was leaving.

"Excuse me. I've never been here before. How do you order?"

He chuckled. "You're in for a treat. Best burgers around. Make sure you know what you want, then approach the counter." He pointed to a spot. "Then holler it out. When you have your order, you pay for it."

"Thank you," Kat said.

"You're welcome."

"Do you want tater tots or fries, monkey?" She jostled Griffin in her arms.

"Tots."

She knew Griffin only wanted cheese and ketchup

on her burger, but Kat felt in the mood to try something new. The combination of grilled onions, banana peppers, and cranberry jam sounded too good to turn down. "Let's do this." She held up her hand and Griffin slapped it.

She stepped up to the counter, called out their order, and hoped she'd done it correctly. She must have, because less than fifteen minutes later a tray laden with their food was set on the counter in front of her. The woman must have known she was new and directed her to the cash register, then stated she would get their drinks when the food order was paid. This straightforward approach looked hectic but worked.

Kat set Griffin on the floor, with a warning to stick close to her, picked up the tray, and made their way to the register. As soon as the woman behind the counter turned toward them, Kat was glad she'd set the tray on the counter, or else she would have dropped it, as her heart thudded in her chest almost painfully.

Dark curly blond hair framed a pair of dazzling brown eyes. She'd never had a reaction to a woman like this before. Underneath the woman's make-up, Kat could see a faint dusting of freckles that enhanced her beauty. *Snap out of it.*

"What can I get you to drink?" As the woman rang up the items on their tray, Kat couldn't get her mouth to work.

Griffin reached up and placed her hands on the counter. "Milk."

The woman leaned over the counter. "Hello there, sweetie. Milk?"

"Please."

"Well, aren't you a cutie." She retrieved Griffin's milk. "And what can I get for you…or should your daughter order for you?" Her eyes twinkled.

That pulled Kat out of her stupor. "Niece. She's my niece and I'll have—water's fine. Water." Kat cursed her lack of suave.

The woman held back a snicker. "Water it is." She left and came back a moment later. "That will be fifteen forty-eight."

Without a word, Kat dug in her pocket for her wallet and handed over a twenty. As the woman accepted the money, Kat noticed a rainbow bracelet on her wrist. It looked like the same one Briley wore that she received when she volunteered at Garriety's LGBTQ summer fundraiser a few summers back. Though, not a clear indication that she was gay, it was a positive sign. "Keep the change."

"Thanks."

Quickly, Kat picked up the tray, spun around, then spotted an empty table in the corner and directed Griffin to hurry to it. After Kat set the tray on the table, she jerked around at the touch on her arm.

"Sorry," the woman said, and took a step back. "I thought she might need a booster seat."

"No problem. Really." Kat smiled, hoping she didn't look deranged. "Thank you." Seeing her out from behind the counter added to Kat's distress. The woman stood a head shorter than her and the jeans and Polo showed off the woman's curves to perfection. *Breathe, Kat, breathe.*

"You're welcome, Kat." She must have noticed Kat's startled look. "Your name's on your shirt." She looked to the stitched name on Kat's shirt pocket.

Kat looked down. So it was. She would have to thank Kyle for suggesting that. *Get it together.* Good lord, Briley had more game than she did. "If you know my name, it's only fair I know yours." That she could complete a sentence made her proud. It was a start.

The smile that blossomed on the woman's face and the emergence of two adorable dimples was almost Kat's undoing. "Dylan. I hope you enjoy your meal. Someone's already started." The twinkle in her eyes came back as she turned and walked away.

When Kat registered what Dylan said, she turned to find Griffin standing on her tip toes eating a tater tot.

"Sorry, monkey." Kat removed Griffin's backpack. "Let's get you set up." She felt eyes on her but chose to focus on eating and helping Griffin. After pouring Griffin's milk into a sippy cup, she cut Griffin's burger into smaller bits. When Griffin started eating, Kat sat and picked up her burger. With the first bite, she moaned as the flavors exploded in her mouth. Good grief. The burger was amazing. She knew it was a home run when Griffin didn't look up from her plate.

"Good?"

Griffin nodded, ketchup smeared across her face. Kat snapped a picture and sent it to Briley and Leah. A moment later, she received a picture of a fancy decorated table with candles and wine. Briley knew how to step up her game when needed. After all, she had gotten Leah.

All through their meal, she tried to keep her eyes from straying to Dylan, who she figured was around her age, but failed five times out of ten. A couple of times she caught her staring back.

When she caught and held Dylan's gaze, a warmth enveloped her that she'd never felt before. It was always nice to catch the attention of a beautiful woman. Besides, a couple of smiles wasn't enough to turn her whole world upside down. Dylan was working; of course she smiled and treated all her customers in a friendly manner. That was good business sense.

A whimper drew her back to Griffin, who, as she watched in horror, spit out onto the table what she'd eaten. With a quick glance at the table top, Kat started at the remains of a banana pepper that Griffin had swiped from Kat's plate.

"Monkey?" Kat jumped up from the table, drawing the attention of the people seated around her. Fear washed through her at the sheer look of panic on Griffin's face. *Fuck.*

Griffin had her tongue sticking out and wiped it off with her napkin.

"Shoot." Kat picked up her milk and screwed off the top. "Drink this. It'll make you feel better." Kat lifted Griffin into her arms, then sat down with Griffin in her lap. Tears were visible in the little one's eyes. "Drink." Griffin grabbed the cup, and Kat was sure she'd gotten more on herself then in her mouth. She picked up her phone, googled whether it would be harmful to her, and breathed a sigh of relief when read it wouldn't.

She looked up from her phone when a shadow passed above them.

"Is she okay?" Dylan set another small glass of milk on the table. "It won't hurt her. I'm almost positive she was more freaked out by the taste as much as the heat."

And the butterflies were back. "Monkey, you okay?" To both of their surprise, Griffin turned in Kat's lap and held her arms up for Dylan to hold her. "No, monkey, she's working."

"I can take five." Dylan waited for Kat's nod of

approval before lifting a willing Griffin into her arms. "There, there." She patted Griffin on the back. "You're okay. Just a bit of a surprise." Dylan scooted the booster seat over and sat across from Kat, rubbing circles on Griffin's back, who had snuggled into her chest.

Kat stared at her in awe. Her little wingwoman had more moves than she did. For Dylan to be so comfortable with Griffin, she'd either been around kids a lot or she had some of her own. Kat opened her mouth to say something when her phone rang. She glanced down at the screen and groaned. Of course it was Briley. It's like she had a sixth sense for these things. That's the last person she wanted to talk to, but knew she had to answer, or Briley and Leah would worry. "Hello."

"Hey, we wanted to Facetime with Griffin now, because we won't get a chance to later."

Kat fumbled with her napkin and ignored the look Dylan gave her. "Oh, I don't know. I'm sure you'll have time later."

"No, we won't. We just got engaged. If we're interrupted tonight, it better be because something's on fire or someone's dying. Evan's spending the night with a friend," Briley said. "Is everything okay?"

"Fine. Fine."

"You're acting weird."

"We're still at the café."

"Mommy. Mama," Griffin said, making grabby hands for the phone.

Kat sighed. "Okay, Bri. She ate a piece of my banana pepper and is upset. One of the workers here is comforting her. She's okay."

A pause, then another voice came over the line. "That's odd. Griff usually doesn't like strangers," Leah said.

Kat ignored the comment because she knew Griff didn't like strangers, switched to Facetime, and turned the phone around to Griffin, who grabbed it. "Mama."

"Hello, sweet pea. Mommy is here with me. Are you okay?"

Griffin almost dropped the phone, but Dylan grabbed it. "It hurt."

"I'm sure it did, but it looks like you made a new friend," Leah said.

Griffin nodded.

"I'm Dylan."

"Briley, Kat's sister, and my fiancé, Leah. Nice to meet you."

"You as well," Dylan said.

"Goodnight, Griff," Briley said. "Don't give Aunt Kat a hard time."

"No."

"Love you, sweet pea," Leah said.

"Love you, Mommy."

Kat accepted the phone back and slipped it in her pocket, even as Griffin snuggled deeper into Dylan's arms. Kat jumped up and gathered all their trash, never taking her eyes off the pair sitting at the table. As she walked back to the table, her phone vibrated. A text and photo from Briley. The photo showed both grinning at the camera and giving her a thumb up.

Wow. She's gorgeous and Griffin likes her. A win-win.

Kat rolled her eyes and slipped the phone back in her pocket. When she made it back to the table, Griffin was asleep. "I'm sorry she dragged you away from your work but thank you." She settled her hand on the table.

"Not a problem. She's a little sweetie. It's not

every day you try your first banana pepper."

Kat buried her head in her hands. "I'm a terrible aunt."

"What? No." Dylan touched Kat's arm and Kat lifted her face. "She's fine. Surprised, but fine. Trying new things is a part of life. Granted, it might be a while before she tries one again, but lesson learned."

Dylan then laughed low, the sound like music to Kat's ears. What was wrong with her? These types of things didn't happen to her. Meeting a stranger and feeling an instant connection. She'd met her last girlfriend through a mutual friend, and it took weeks for her to be comfortable. There weren't enough hours in the day for working, let alone a relationship.

"You're right," was all Kat said.

"Dylan," someone called out. "We could use you back here."

Dylan smiled. "That's my cue." Kat jumped up and accepted Griffin back. "We loved having you two. Come back any time." Her hand lingered on Kat's arm.

Kat gulped, then nodded. "We will."

"Good night."

"Night."

On the way home, she kept stealing glances at Griffin in the back seat, who slept soundly curled up in her car seat, Bob, her stuffed giraffe, firmly in hand. She'd made it through her first fear induced event with Griffin by herself. If that's what it meant to be a mother, she could, maybe, handle that. Mostly it was fun times, temper tantrums, and yoga, but Kat wouldn't trade her time with Griffin for anything.

As she pulled her truck into the garage, her thoughts strayed to Dylan. She wasn't so shallow to only be interested in a woman for her looks, but Dylan also showed a side of compassion and empathy for Griffin that you didn't see every day. That was incredibly sexy.

She stroked her hands down her face when Griffin whimpered. Shaking the thoughts of Dylan out of her mind, she got out and opened Griffin's door. When Griffin clung to her neck, Kat drew in a deep breath. This is what mattered. Not an interaction with a woman she probably wouldn't see again. The burgers were good, but she couldn't see herself driving to get one that often.

Chapter Four

With a groan, Dylan collapsed in her driver's seat after starting the car. She reversed out of the parking lot of the Burger Café and headed toward NightCrawlers, a bar and grill in downtown Garriety, for drinks with Haley. It turned into a long day, but she would do it again if her cousin asked. The two hundred dollars in tips plus her wage for the day didn't hurt either.

Forty minutes later, she was seated with a Sprite, listening to Haley fill her in on the dealings at the hotel. Her eyes scanned the large space and she did a double take when a woman in the corner caught her eye. For a split second she thought it was Kat and felt a bit disappointed it wasn't. Their interactions earlier had thrown her off her game but having Kat's complete attention was a nice treat.

When she had taken her break at the restaurant, she'd googled Kat's business. The business was new and in Garriety. She also tapped on the icon that would lead her to Kat's Instagram page. It wasn't at all what she expected. There were posts about her business, but most of the pictures were of her niece and her ferret. What hadn't surprised her, but was a nice confirmation, were the photos of Kat at Pride last year. In the post underneath one of the photos, Kat had talked about her coming out experience. How lovely, Kat had answered every question under her post.

Haley snapped fingers in front of her face, then turned to see what held Dylan's attention. "If you want to talk to her, I won't mind."

"No. She reminded me of someone."

"I see." Haley sipped her cosmopolitan. "Somebody new?" Dylan recounted her meeting Kat. "Kat?" She bit her lip. "Did you get her last name?"

"Her shirt said Anderson Tiny Homes. Do you know her?" Dylan leaned forward, more eager then she wanted to admit, to hearing what Haley had to say. Cyber stalking could only tell you so much.

Haley grinned. "I don't know her, but I know of her and her sister, Briley. A woman that used to work the front desk at the hotel had a crush on Kat at one point. Kat turned her down when she asked her out."

That wasn't what she expected. First impression told her Kat was a player. "Didn't you tell me that your sister said Briley was the name of the woman that Easton had a crush on?" Ashley, Haley's sister, worked at Brew and Bake, the bakery that Easton owned.

"Yup. She was going to ask her out, but by that time Briley started dating someone else…Leah is her name. Always this close." She held up her thumb and forefinger close together.

Dylan took another sip of her Sprite. "Briley and Leah are getting married."

Haley looked up from her drink. "Since when?"

Dylan explained what happened with Griffin. "She introduced Leah as her fiancée."

Haley held her glass up. "To love."

Dylan rolled her eyes but held her glass up anyway. "To love."

"Don't be so cynical. It's out there. Kat's a looker, I'll give you that."

"She doesn't strike you as a player?" Dylan sipped her drink.

"Kat?" Haley shrugged. "Not really. She's got that whole hot butch thing going on, but she can also rock a dress. I think she just presents herself well."

That wasn't the exact impression Dylan had of her. "She seemed a bit nervous tonight."

"Really? How so?"

Dylan went on to explain everything that transpired.

"Sounds like she saw something in you that interested her." Haley grinned over the rim of her drink.

"Don't be silly. We barely even talked and how would she even know I'm bi?" Dylan waved her off.

"What's to be silly about? You're a beautiful woman and those dimples could bring about world peace. Don't sell yourself so short. You have a lot to offer someone and if she noticed your bracelet, that would have at the least told her you were an ally."

"I suppose. I hate dating." At least she did now. When younger, it was a lot easier. Now it was hard to tell whether someone wanted a one-night stand or happy ever after. At this point in her life, she couldn't date anyone indecisive.

"When was the last time you went out? Been laid? What, four or five weeks?" Haley accused.

"Something like that," Dylan mumbled, downing the rest of her Sprite. Truth was, she hadn't had sex with anyone for over two years. Between her jobs, and taking care of Emma, there wasn't time and she wasn't a one-night stand kind of woman.

The waitress set an order of fried mushrooms in the middle of the table. Haley dipped one in the sauce. "Mmm," she wiped her mouth, "that's good. I was going to ask. You know the gala is in a few weeks?"

"Of course." It was an opportunity for the business people in Garriety to get together and raise money for charity and not an event she would ever be invited to.

"Gayle is catering the event and could use some extra hands. I told her I'd ask you. With setup and clean up, she's offering two hundred and fifty dollars."

Dylan drowned a mushroom in the sauce then plopped it in her mouth. She'd worked for Gayle, Haley's older sister, before and there was no way she could turn down that kind of money or the leftover food Gayle allowed them to split and take home. "Just tell me when and where."

"Awesome. I'm going to be there too. It'll be great. I'll have her send you an email with all the details."

They finished off the mushrooms.

"Who knows," Haley said, "Kat might be there, and you can ask her out." Haley wiggled her eyebrows.

The thought scared her more than she was willing to admit. Not because she feared for Kat to see her working the event but because the thought of Kat being a guest meant there was no way she'd ask her out. They were on two different playing fields. At least money wise, and people that had plenty of money never seemed to understand the ones that didn't. She dated one woman that told her if she worked harder and tried harder, she wouldn't be struggling. Dylan had thrown her drink in the woman's face and stormed off. It hadn't been one of her finer moments.

"We'll see." She glanced at her watch. "I hate to cut this short, but I have to stop at the store before going home."

"Sure." Haley stood and embraced Dylan, kissing her on the cheek. "Give my love to Iris and Emma. I'll see you at work tomorrow."

"I will."

Marketplace usually wasn't her first stop, but it was on the way home and she could get everything on the list.

Twenty minutes into her shopping trip, she'd marked off everything on her list. Almost on its own accord, her cart took her to the toy section, or more importantly, the Lego aisle. She grabbed a couple of the Lego Minifigures blind bags and threw them in the cart. There were a few figures Emma didn't have yet, and she loved the mystery of what she would get. All her multiples she would give to a boy whose physical therapy was scheduled the same time as hers.

While wheeling her cart out of the aisle, she spotted a DC super hero girls doll display and noticed a new Wonder Woman one that Emma didn't have. Without a second thought, she picked it up and put it in the cart. Dylan knew she spoiled her daughter, but Emma was a well-adjusted little girl and rarely asked for anything when they were out. And with the extra money from tonight and the upcoming catering gig, she had a little extra cash to splurge on her daughter. Besides, tomorrow Emma was going horseback riding, and even though she knew it would be fun, it always wore Emma out and left her exhausted.

Thankfully, there were plenty of self-checkouts open and she was out of the store thirty minutes after entering. The drive home was quiet, Dylan opting not to turn the radio on. Her thoughts strayed to Kat and her cute niece of their own accord. She remembered the first time Emma ate something hot and had the same reaction Griffin did.

The connection she'd felt toward Kat was

unexpected and nice, but, at the moment, unwanted. That's why she hadn't mentioned it to Haley, who believed in true love. Kat was exactly her type, with her long legs and toned physique. That, coupled with her obvious love for her niece, left Dylan with a warm and fuzzy feeling. A bit of flirting never hurt anyone, and the interest was obvious in Kat's eyes.

She'd noticed Kat as soon as she had walked in. It was hard not to. Kat cut quite the figure. When Kat was paying for their food, it had taken all of Dylan's restraint not to reach across the counter and run her fingers through Kat's hair. She wondered if it was as soft as it looked.

She shook off her foolish thoughts after pulling into the garage. Her mother held the door open for her as she started unloading the bags. After setting the last load down, she turned to her mother, seeing her pursed lips. Dylan narrowed her eyes. "What? Is Emma okay?"

Iris tilted her head. "Emma's fine. Been asleep for a few hours."

The look her mother directed at her didn't mean anything good. That look was the one Iris gave them when she wanted something. "Mom?" Without waiting for an answer, she started unpacking the food.

After a few minutes, Iris spoke quietly. "I haven't seen a smile like that on your face for a long time."

Dylan stopped with a bag of green beans in her hand. "What?"

"Your cousin called me today after she closed up. Said you had a friendly conversation with a customer… female." Iris joined her in unpacking the groceries.

"Of course she did." Figured Macy wouldn't keep her mouth shut. "I helped a customer and her niece who ate a banana pepper and they were both freaking out." She shrugged. "I helped them out. That's all it was."

"All it was? Macy seemed to think there was more to it. She straight?"

With a sigh, Dylan continued unpacking the groceries. "Yes, Mom, that's all it was. I forgot how nice it is to share a connection with someone, even if for a fleeting moment…and no, she's not straight. I might have checked out her Instagram page."

"Might have?"

"Okay, I did."

"So, not someone you would date?"

Dylan leaned back against the counter and crossed her arms. "Mom, we've talked about this." She closed her eyes and pinched the bridge of her nose. "I doubt I will ever see her again. Hundreds of people eat there every day, and I was only helping out."

"Macy did say she had never seen her there before."

"She told me that as well."

"So, not someone you would date?" Iris asked again.

If she was honest with herself, if Kat had asked, she would have said yes, but their moment had already passed. Besides, instant connections weren't real. Even she and Ian had to work at it. "I'm not looking for a relationship. I'm not even sure I would have time for a new friendship. I barely have time for Haley. If it wasn't for us working together, I would never see her. A romantic relationship would take up too much of my time, but I might be able to juggle another friend." Probably not, but she wanted to appease her mom.

"I understand that, sweetheart."

"But?"

Iris smiled and kissed Dylan's cheek. "No but.

Your happiness is my number one priority."

"I am happy. Do I want more, yes, but not today." Both stayed silent as they continued unpacking.

"Emma will love these. Did you do that well in tips?" Iris picked up the items Dylan bought for Emma.

Dylan went on to explain the catering gig, then stifled a yawn behind her hand. "I'm going to take a shower and relax. Night."

"Good night."

One quick shower, and a cup of tea later, Dylan lay curled up in bed staring at the ceiling. A sliver of light from the moon broke through the curtain and painted the ceiling in color. She needed to sleep, but her mind was a jumbled mess. Everything bombarded her at once.

Her relationship with Ian seemed ideal, but she always felt like something was missing. It was good, and they loved each other, but it never felt complete, even when Emma came along. She wanted an all-encompassing feeling, something not felt with Ian. They'd talked about it once, but in the end, decided to make it work and she didn't regret it. Not even for a second.

Maybe someday she could have it all with someone new. It was something she dreamed about but would never tell her family because they would try to set her up. When the right time came, she would know it, and she knew now wasn't the right time.

Chapter Five

Kat skimmed her hand across the cabinets in McGovern's, Briley's go to hardware store, on Saturday morning. She'd decided to tag along when Briley mentioned she needed to pick up a few things for her house over breakfast. Which was code for 'she needed some things for her Christmas decorations'. Leah was a saint for putting up with Briley's Christmas obsession.

Where various lengths of wood and some miscellaneous items filled Briley's cart, Kat's cart only contained a couple of light fixtures for her house and a few boards for shelves she wanted to put up in her office for her collection of Harley Quinn figurines. This could've waited until next week, considering she'd already agreed to accompany Evan to buy flowers for his planned garden, but she wanted to spend time with Briley. Work kept her busy and they hadn't had a lot of time together.

A few weeks had passed since her and Griffin's trip to the Burger Café and she'd be lying if she denied that Dylan hadn't crossed her mind during that time. She'd tried to look her up on social media but couldn't find anything.

"Aunt Kat."

Kat looked across the aisle where an excited Griffin waved at her, wearing a miniature tool belt, almost the same as Briley's. Griffin would have run toward her, but Briley had a firm grip on the back of her shirt. Kat smiled and made her way across the aisle to join them, then knelt next to Griffin.

She made a motion for Griffin to turn. "Wow, monkey. Look at you. Just like Mama."

Griffin bobbed her head, then tilted it back to look up at Briley, who beamed. Motherhood suited her. "Yup."

Briley bent and scooped Griffin up. "We're a team." She raised her hand for Griffin to slap, then they both turned to Kat. "Team Anderson."

"I'll high-five to that." It had surprised Kat when Leah had made the decision to take their last name and to change Griffin's once she and Briley were married the following year. Leah had explained it was a new beginning for them both. Evan had chosen to keep Kathy, his other mother's, last name and at first, he had a hard time with them changing Griffin's last name. He felt like they were erasing his mom and step-mom, Lilith, from Griffin's life after they died, but Leah had quickly assured him that wasn't the case. Briley and family had gone away last weekend to visit Madison, Leah's daughter, and when they came back, Evan had changed his mind. Kat never asked what occurred during their time away and neither Leah or Briley had volunteered the information, but Kat was glad everything worked out.

Kat took a willing Griffin in her arms and glanced to her left, then did a double take. Not twenty feet from her was Dylan. Even after only meeting her once, she would know those dimples anywhere. Her hair was tucked up under a Meerkat baseball cap and she had on a pair of ripped jeans and a long-sleeve blue Henley paired with a pair of sandals. Her toenails were painted a deep red. She mumbled to herself while looking at the light fixtures. She was the cutest thing Kat had ever seen.

    Kat jerked away when Briley whispered in her ear.

    "Is that the woman from the Burger Café?" She whistled.

    "Shut up," Kat hissed and set Griffin down on the floor. When she looked back up, Dylan was looking at her with a crooked grin. Kat returned the smile and hoped it looked friendly, then turned back to a grinning Briley, who lifted her hand and waved at Dylan. Kat kept her gaze fixed on Briley.

    "Must you act like that?" Briley always did this to her. It was so embarrassing. Although, considering what she put Briley through concerning Leah, she guessed she deserved it. Karma was a bitch.

    Briley lifted Griffin into her cart. "We're going to look at the flooring. Leah wants to redo the bathrooms in the house. Go talk with her." She glanced in Kat's cart. "You're a professional; you can help her before someone else does." She nudged Kat with her shoulder. "Go, or else."

    Kat kept her eyes glued to the spot Briley had left, took a deep breath, then turned her cart toward Dylan, who still stood by the light fixtures. She could do this. She was an adult, for goodness sake. Why was she getting so worked up over this? Dylan was only a woman. A beautiful woman, but a woman nonetheless. She had just made up her mind to walk up to her when an older woman stepped up beside Dylan with a light fixture in hand and they started talking.

    Well, how anticlimactic, Kat thought. When the older lady looked in her direction, Kat froze, but quickly lost her nerve, and turned to walk away.

She couldn't do this. How Briley had done this with Leah, she had no clue. She now realized what an ass she was toward Briley concerning Leah. Fortunately, everything worked out.

"Kat, I thought that was you."

Kat stopped her cart and groaned at hearing Mrs. Hanlin's voice. It sounded suspiciously like it came from the direction where Dylan was standing. One thing she quickly learned when she moved to Garriety was that one never ignored Mrs. Hanlin, her and Briley's neighbor. In all honesty, Kat did like her, and Mrs. Hanlin made the most scrumptious sausage casserole around. Being invited to one of her brunches was the highlight of anyone's week. She plastered a smile on, then turned. Sure enough, Mrs. Hanlin was standing close by the other two women. Kat squinted, noticing the fake smile. This was all Briley's doing. She didn't know how, but it was. She knew it.

"Mrs. Hanlin." Kat approached her and leaned on the handle of the cart. "What brings you here today? You know if you ever need anything, Briley or I would be happy to assist you." She could feel Dylan and the other woman's eyes on her but was determined to not look in their direction.

Mrs. Hanlin patted her cheek. "Aren't you a dear? I thought Briley was a charmer, but I think you have her beat by a mile."

"Stop, you flatterer." She winked at Mrs. Hanlin, who laughed.

"You're this far away from being my favorite." She held her thumb and forefinger a breath apart.

Kat clutched her hands to her chest. "Don't tell Briley."

"Don't tell Briley what?"

Kat jumped to her right, almost knocking into Dylan when Briley spoke from directly behind her. "I'm sorry." She held out her hands, but Dylan was standing still, then jerked her hands back, turned and glared at an innocent looking Briley.

"Nothing, dear," Mrs. Hanlin said, then turned her attention on a talkative Griffin. "Well, Griffin, don't you look professional?"

"Sorry about her," Briley said to Dylan. "She can be unreasonably jumpy."

"No harm done." Dylan looked from one to the other.

Kat held herself back from swooning at the sound of Dylan's voice. *Deep breath, Kat. You can do this.*

"I see your daughter suffered no ill effects from her pepper incident," Dylan said.

"She's tougher than she looks." Briley stuck out her hand. "Let me formally introduce myself. Briley Anderson."

"Dylan Lake, and this is my mom, Iris."

"Nice to meet you both," Briley said. "I can only imagine this one," she hiked her thumb in Kat's direction, "freaking out about it."

"She handled herself well," Dylan said. "It's always scary when something like that happens."

"Thank you." Kat wanted to run as far as possible away from this situation. Dylan was being polite, but not overly friendly and she feared she'd misread everything at the diner. After all, they hadn't seen each other in weeks.

"I see you have some light fixtures in your cart," Iris said, looking at Kat. "Maybe you could help me decide what to get for my living room. I don't want to spend a lot of money, but it needs to be replaced."

"I mean…sure." Kat took Iris's phone, then looked at pictures of her living room while Briley talked with Dylan and Mrs. Hanlin. She kept an ear trained on them but couldn't make out what they were saying. It only took them a few minutes to pick a new light fixture. Kat stuffed her hands in her pockets and rocked back on her heels while Briley wrapped up the conversation.

Iris touched Dylan's arm. "We need to get going."

"We do." Dylan nodded. "It was nice meeting all of you." She bopped Griffin on the nose, then turned to Kat. "And nice seeing you again, Kat."

"I know…no…yes. Wait." Kat ran a hand through her hair. "You too." She coughed. "It was nice seeing you again too." God, could she be any more of a loser? Dylan's chuckle made her feel even lower and she remained tongue-tied when they walked off and got in line to check out.

Mrs. Hanlin tapped the bottom of Kat's jaw. "You can relax, dear, they're gone. All in all, you did good." She had a knowing smile. "She's nice. I would need to get to know her more before I approve. Of course."

"It's not like that. This is only the second time I've met her." She bit her lip. "There isn't anything for you to approve of. I don't even know if she's gay." This whole crush could be for naught.

"Well, dear, only one way to know. Ask her out." Mrs. Hanlin kissed Griffin on the cheek and walked away.

"I never thought I would live to see Kat Anderson freak out," Briley said with way too much amusement in her voice.

"Like you have room to talk, 'Ms. I Ran from the Woman I Liked and Didn't Talk to Her for Months.'"

"Oh, man." Briley laughed, holding her sides. "I know you like her because you always act like a smart ark when you have your serious face on."

Kat frowned. "What did you say?"

Briley glanced at Griffin, then back to Kat. "Smart 'ark'. We're trying not to cuss around little ears. She picks up on everything. Everything, Kat. Leah said if Griffin picked up on my cussing, I would have to sleep on the couch for a week, but if she picked up on the four-letter word that starts with an f, then I wouldn't get any for a month. A month, Kat. So, I've taken to substituting words." She looked horrified.

She believed it. Leah was an amazing woman, but strict when it came to certain things. "And do I want to even know what word you use for that particular four-letter word?"

"Fork."

"I can forking believe it." They held it in for a moment before both burst out laughing. They were mostly ignored but a few people turned in their direction, including Dylan, who quickly turned back around. "Well then, let's get the fork out of here and get something to eat."

When they were loading the truck, Briley turned to her with a serious look. "Next time you see her, you should ask her out. Life's short and you deserve to be happy. Don't deny yourself."

Kat loaded their last bags into the truck. "Damn, when did you get so smart?"

"Damn." They both whipped their heads around and stared at Griffin, who repeated the word again and again. "Damn. Damn. Damn." She laughed and hugged Bob close to her chest.

"I'm glad it was you and not me," Briley said,

wiping her brow. "Let's get the fork out of here because I can't wait to tell Leah all about this."

Kat hung her head. Leah didn't have no sex to dangle in front of her but could be creative when she needed to be. One thing for sure, if she ran into Dylan again, she would bite the bullet and ask her out, or at least, that was the plan.

Chapter Six

Dylan hummed and pushed her cart down the aisle of Hancock's Nursery. Katie, her boss, asked her to pick up the plants for the hotel's front entrance since it was a slow day. She'd readily agreed and with Katie's truck and money in hand, she'd quickly left.

The mulch and edging were already secured in the truck, along with the plant food and other accessories. She wanted to get that out of the way before she took her time looking at the flowers. Gardening was her one true passion and she got to go wild with it at the hotel. Plus Katie went above and beyond and always paid her extra when she did the landscaping for the hotel. Each flower was special, and she loved teaching others about them. Her dad shared the same passion and she hoped Emma would in the future.

After picking up a bucket of cornflowers, she saw a familiar someone standing with a young man by the tulips. The last time she saw Kat was a couple of weeks ago. Today Kat wore a pair of skinny jeans, Converse shoes, and a Garriety Science Center t-shirt. Her hair was spiked and as she watched, Kat raised her sunglasses and pushed them up and into her hair. Sexy didn't even convey how Kat looked. What an attractive woman.

The decision to help them was taken out of her hands when Kat looked up and locked eyes with her.

Dylan pushed her cart over to them.

"Hello again, Kat." Dylan pushed a piece of hair behind her ear. The way Kat always made her nervous was quite the inconvenience.

"It's good to see you again, Dylan."

"Our third meeting." Kat's bout of shyness charmed Dylan.

"Good." Evan clapped his hands. "You two know each other." He held out his hand. "I'm Evan, Kat's nephew."

"Dylan. Nice to meet you, Evan."

"Ah…do you know anything about flowers?" Evan asked.

"Evan, she's obviously busy." Kat flicked her hand at Dylan's cart.

"Not that busy." She looked toward the flowers. "What are you looking for?" The words were out of her mouth before she dared to think about them. The last thing needed was to spend more time with Kat.

"I want to plant a flower garden and Aunt Kat thought it would be a good project for the both of us, but…" He looked around them.

"A bit daunting." This she could do. "How big of a garden?"

They both looked out of their element. "Nothing too big. Mom has her garden in the front yard and Briley has her vegetable garden in the backyard and they both made it clear I'm not to mess with either one of them. So, we're doing it at her house." He touched Kat's arm.

"I've marked off a two foot by ten-foot section in the front yard," Kat said, slipping her hands in her front pockets.

"Full sun?" Dylan asked.

"Yes."

"Okay. What about colors? Are you looking for fragrance? Something to attract butterflies? Or something you could cut in a pinch for a date?"

Evan grinned. "The date one would be awesome. Flowers are so expensive in the store."

"Follow me." They walked two rows over. "You're getting started and almost everyone grows daylily because they're easy and require little maintenance. They're personally one of my favorites and come in a variety of colors." Dylan stopped and pointed out several types. "They are most associated with funerals because they symbolize the soul of the departed, but they also symbolize humility and devotion. That's why they are considered the thirtieth anniversary flower." The look of awe on both their faces was a welcome surprise. Evan grabbed two different colored daylily and added them to the cart.

"What are these?" Evan tapped a display.

"Ah." Dylan picked up a container. "These are hydrangea. They're gorgeous, but it's a bush so you need to plant them away from your other flowers. They symbolize emotion and understanding." Evan took the one out of her hand and put it in their cart.

"So." Kat tapped the side of her cart. "What symbolizes romance?"

Dylan crooked her finger and they followed. "Peony. They come in a variety of colors, but I've always been partial to pink. They can also mean prosperity, good fortune, a happy marriage, riches, honor, and compassion, along with bashfulness."

Kat looked at Evan. "I don't think your mom has any of these. Let's get some for Briley and Leah."

"What would you give someone you liked?" Evan

asked, a blush coloring his cheeks.

"Well, that depends on what you want to convey. Aster is for patience, elegance, and daintiness. Calla lily for magnificence and beauty. Carnations have a few symbols. Pink is for the love of a woman or mother. White, innocence and pure love. Of course, you can't go wrong with roses, but different colors have different meanings and roses need their own space as well."

"What about the roses?" Kat leaned against the wall and stared intently at Dylan.

Dylan had to admit she enjoyed having all of Kat's attention on her.

"Yes," Evan said, coming back and setting some asters in the cart.

"You both should know that red is the lover's rose and signifies enduring passion." They both nodded. "White is for humility and innocence. Yellow expresses friendship and joy. Pink is for gratitude, appreciation, and admiration. Orange for enthusiasm and desire. White lilac and purple roses represent enchantment and love at first sight. The different number of stems in a bouquet can also express specific sentiments."

"That's awesome," Evan said. "Let's get some red roses." Kat nodded, and he sped off.

"You're not bored?" Dylan loved talking about flowers but knew people could get easily bored.

"Not at all. It really is fascinating. I knew different flowers had different meanings, but I never gave it much thought. Now I'm wondering what I've been conveying to Leah all these months." At Dylan's confusion, she went on and explained about taking up so much of Briley's time.

Dylan's voice sounded amused. "I'm sure she appreciated them, but when you put your heart into it, it does make a difference what you're trying to say to someone. It's special when someone takes the time to express themselves through flowers, but most people don't take the time to dig deeper."

"Your love of flowers is evident," Kat said. "Like my and Briley's love of cosplaying. Everyone has something they're proud of and interested in."

"You don't think it's silly?"

"Of course not. The world would be a boring place if everyone liked and enjoyed the same things. Life's too short. Enjoy what makes you happy."

"That's a nice attitude to have. It's refreshing." Dylan leaned forward on her cart.

"I'm not going to give my time to people who are purposely being an asshole. I don't have time for that."

It was her third meeting with Kat, and she wondered if it was some type of sign. She was definitely attracted to Kat and would like to get to know her better. It was a thought that almost paralyzed her. She did not have time for these types of feelings. Not now.

"I'm back." Evan's arms were laden down with several containers.

"My, but you're going all in." Dylan kept her mouth shut at the cost adding up in their cart. She hoped one day she could enter a store like this and buy whatever she wanted. It was nice that they could, and they looked so happy doing it.

"Why not," Evan said and looked at Kat.

"Why not." Kat agreed. "Now, I'm sure this isn't everything we need. Do you have the time to assist us with everything else or should we wave down an employee?"

Dylan glanced at her watch. "I've got a bit of time." She motioned for them to go in front of her and gave suggestions of what they might need. When they had three carts full, she glanced at them, then Kat glanced at Evan.

"I hope you brought your debit card." Kat smirked in Evan's direction.

Dylan held in a snicker when Evan's eyes widened, then he grinned and whipped out a card from his back pocket. "I bet you thought I would make you pay for everything. I'll have you know I'm responsible." There was a moment of silence between them. Dylan wasn't sure what was going on, but it looked intense.

"If you're sure?" Kat finally asked.

The look that crossed his face was so fleeting, Dylan would have missed it if she hadn't been looking. Then the look vanished in a flash.

"I'm sure. We may not be able to beat Briley in the Christmas competition, but we're so going to kick their asses when it comes to gardens." He sounded confident.

Dylan snickered at the expression on Kat's face. "Not confident, Kat?"

Kat took out her phone, unlocked it, brought up her photos then handed the phone to her. Dylan looked down and her eyes widened. The vegetable garden could rival any magazine spread. Everything was so precise and flourishing. She swiped through and stopped on the flowers in the front yard. Though there was a limited variety, everything was done to precision also. The house was gorgeous as well.

"Good luck." Dylan looked at her watch. "I need to get going." Kat looked like she wanted to say something but only nodded. Dylan left them looking at their phones and pointing out different varieties.

Once she went through the checkout and was

sitting in the truck, she gave herself a moment of pause to ponder the experience. There was no denying she felt a pull toward Kat, but she couldn't gauge the other woman's interest.

With a groan, she rested her head back on the seat. Her attraction toward Kat didn't change anything, though. There was no way she had time for a girlfriend. Friends would be pushing it. And she wasn't sure Kat would be interested in her if she knew how they lived. She wasn't ashamed of their house, but it was small and could use a lot of TLC. She shook her head and cleared her thoughts. The last thing she needed was to start putting words in Kat's mouth. She didn't know how Kat would react and she couldn't hold what others thought about her against Kat, who had done nothing but be nice. She owed at least that much to Kat. Besides, there were more important things to worry about besides a fleeting crush on a woman she only ever saw in passing.

Kat slipped the rag out of her back pocket and wiped her face and neck off before accepting the glass of iced tea Evan held out. She was surprised when Evan had agreed to pay for part of the flowers, but he had insisted. Leah had received the check for the sale of Kathy and Lilith's house the previous week. All the furniture and knick-knacks were put into a temperature-controlled storage facility for when Evan got his own place and when Griffin was older. Evan and Griffin split the check received for the house and it was deposited into each of their bank accounts. It was a sizable profit, but she knew Evan was a responsible kid. Kat was glad this was something he decided to spend some of his money on. There could be worse things for him to settle his focus on instead of flowers.

"This is going to be great," Evan said, sitting down beside her.

"You better believe it." Besides the space they already designated to the flower garden, Evan had chosen a spot near the road for the hydrangea. They decided to plant the roses in the backyard. At one point they noticed Briley across the street staring at them, but after a text from Evan, Leah had come out and dragged Briley back inside.

"Dylan was a big help," Evan said.

It was the first time he had brought her up and Kat was hoping he wouldn't. The passion Dylan expressed when she was talking about flowers was a welcome surprise. Kat could have listened to her talk all day. Thankfully, Dylan didn't seem bothered by helping them. She was warm and engaging.

"Nice too."

Kat finished her tea. "Do you have a point, Evan?" She rested her arms on her knees. The urge to ask her out was on the tip of her tongue but at the last moment, she'd chickened out; she didn't have time for dating. At least, that's what she would keep telling herself.

"You're thinking about this too much. Just ask her out."

"It's not that easy. I don't know if she's gay."

"Ask her out. If she says no, then you have an answer. She's not gay, or she's not interested. If she says yes, you can bet she's gay and interested. You're making it out to be hard."

Maybe she was. "I don't have time to date."

"Bullshit."

"You sound like Briley. I wish it was that easy for everyone to find their Leah."

"I'll give you that. They're made for each other. I'm glad Mom's happy and I love Briley, but Briley's not the suavest one out there."

Kat laughed. "I don't know about that."

"She's not. She used baking to her advantage and never presented herself to Mom as anything other than herself."

"I can see it now. The next time I see her. Hey, Dylan, I could do your taxes for you."

Evan laughed so hard he fell on the ground. "I bet there is a lot of women who would appreciate that."

She got up, settled beside him, and placed her hands behind her head while Evan talked.

"Mom and Lilith were like that. They fit together like pieces of a puzzle. I know Mom and Briley love Griff, but…I wonder. You know? What would Griff be like if they hadn't died? I honestly…I love our life now, but Griff was their daughter. It's just hard to think about sometimes. I don't want to say it wrong. Do you understand?"

"I do."

"They were so excited for Griffin. We had such a ball decorating Griff's room and Lilith had been so surprised by the finished product. I've got video, but I can't bring myself to watch it. I transferred all my videos and pictures of them to four separate flash drives and SD cards. Not including the Cloud. I don't want to forget them."

"I still can't bring myself to watch the videos I have of my dad. I know I would break down and I'm not sure I could handle that. I know Briley has watched some with Leah, but—"

"Maybe." Evan sat up and so did Kat. "Maybe we could watch some together. My videos and yours."

She stilled his hand that was picking at the grass. "I would really like that. You bring the tissue. I'll supply the snacks."

"Sounds good." He jumped up and wiped his eyes, then held his hand out for Kat, who latched onto it and stood. "Not going to get done sitting around."

"Let's get to it." He was a good kid, or young man. He would turn nineteen in a few weeks. Kat wasn't sure what made him bond with her, but she was glad he did. She loved spending time with Griffin, but cherished the time spent with Evan. He hadn't wanted to enroll in college full-time and the compromise he made with Leah was to take a few classes his first year and take up a hobby. So far, everything had worked out. He was getting into a groove and Kat knew next year, he would be ready for college full-time and they would see less and less of him. She would take these moments as they came.

She lifted another bag of mulch and deposited it on his designated spot. She paused with another bag on her shoulder. Briley used her strengths to her advantage with Leah, but Kat could use someone else's to hers. Tonight, after dinner, she'd sit down and research flower meanings. If she ever worked up the nerve to ask Dylan out, then she would play to Dylan's strengths.

Chapter Seven

Dylan entered the event center three hours before the gala was to start to help set up the tables. To her disappointment, most of the dishes were seafood based and not something Emma liked. There were a few meat dishes she hoped would provide some leftovers to take home. Emma always looked forward to the foods brought home from these events.

"I'll make sure if there is any of the beef dishes left that you get first dibs," Haley said. "I know Emma doesn't like seafood."

"Thanks."

"I'm hoping there are some of those miniature crab cakes and lobster puffs left. Gayle already promised I could have some."

The venue's decorations were lovely. White garland and pink and yellow tulips graced every table. Expensive, but tasteful. It always amazed her how much money was spent on these events that could go directly to charity, but she understood you had to spend money to make it. This event wasn't designated as a benefit for charity, but she knew they always collected donations at the end of the night. And one thing that could be said about the business people of Garriety was that they were generous with their money.

She had a tiny bit of hope that Kat would be here, and she would have the chance to see her all dressed up. It was one thing to see her in jeans and a t-shirt, but she was almost positive Kat would kill formal wear. It was a tossup between whether she would look better in a dress or a suit. She'd seen Kat's arms in a tank top, and now hoped to get a glimpse of her legs in a dress.

"I would say from that grin on your face you're thinking of a certain someone." Haley popped another lobster puff into her mouth.

Dylan rolled her eyes, but the grin remained. "I wouldn't be opposed to seeing Kat in a dress."

"She looks good."

"You did say you saw her in one." Dylan slid the platter of lobster puffs away from Haley's eager hands.

"Last year at the dance right before the Encampment. I do believe she's the type of woman that could pull off any look."

"I believe you're right."

"Ladies," Gayle said, walking up to them. "The doors are going to open in ten minutes, so if you could get behind your stations that would be great."

"Sure thing, Sis," Haley said, as she and Dylan made for their table and got in place. "I kind of had a feeling she wouldn't put me on the crab cake table after I ate three of them in the kitchen."

"Common sense will get you far."

"I'm sure." Haley lifted her tongs. "How about that dead guy at work today?"

Dylan didn't want to think about that. Thank God she wasn't the housekeeper to find him or the one to clean his room. "Brenda was a tad bit dramatic."

"A tad bit? She was flipping out of her mind. For a moment, I had wished it was me because I would have kept my composure, then reality would hit and I'm glad I wasn't the one to find him."

"Me and you both." In the three years she'd

worked at the Town Square, it was only the fourth time they'd found a dead body. One, an older man who had died in his sleep. His wife had blamed the front desk worker because the paramedics weren't quicker getting there, but nothing they could have done would have saved him. Another one, a guy who had taken a pill that his doctor had refused to give him, but he got from his friend and his heart gave out. Another one, a man passing through town who hadn't woken up, an empty pill bottle on the floor by the bed. The coroner had ruled it a suicide. It still creeped her out to clean those rooms, but there wasn't another option.

Most guests were considerate and would tip nicely but there were always those few that believed since she got paid to clean the room, they could trash it. The church groups were the worst. She had one guy that stayed every weekend and loved mini candy bars, but instead of throwing his wrappers in a trash can, he would throw them on the floor. To top it off, he wasn't even a tipper. That wasn't even considering all the borderline crazy people she'd encountered.

"Doors are opening," Haley said.

Dylan stood at the ready in her pressed black pants, crisp white shirt, blue and white checkered bowtie, hair up off her neck. She had worried about the clothes accentuating her excess weight, but Haley had promised her she looked good. Hopefully this night wouldn't drag on when all she wanted was to go home and sleep.

❧❧❧❧

"Tell me again why we're going." Kat smoothed her hands over her stomach as she looked in Briley's bedroom mirror. She didn't have a lot of occasions to dress up since changing jobs, but she still enjoyed it. Tonight, she'd opted for the same black lace, fit and flare dress she'd worn at the dance last year and had to admit she looked good. Since starting the tiny house business, her muscle definition had improved. She'd always been fit but had to admit she liked the new definition.

"If you're through admiring yourself in the mirror, we need to go," Briley said.

Kat narrowed her eyes at Briley. "Don't you look nice."

"This old thing." Briley twirled.

"The suit looks good on you."

Briley had on a pair of cream-colored trousers and a low-cut red camisole with a jacket over top. On her feet, she wore a pair of black kitten heels.

"You look great, Kat." Leah entered the room, wearing a pink A-line dress. Leah and Briley looked good together.

"Thanks, Leah. Besides feeling like a third wheel, I also feel like the weird fourth cousin that no one wants to invite to parties, but they do so out of pity."

"Not fourth," Briley said, waving her hand in the air. "More like first."

"Your reassurance will always mean so much to me, Bri."

"As it should."

They walked into the living room where Evan and Griffin were seated on the couch.

"Don't you all look spiffy." Evan stood and took several pictures.

"You're pretty, Mommy." Griffin bounced on the couch.

"Thank you, sweet pea," Leah said.

"You never answered my question. Why do we have to go?" Kat asked.

Briley rolled her eyes even while accepting Griffin's kisses. "Because the gala is for an important cause and we're both business owners. It will be good to network."

"You can always stay with us," Evan said. "And Disney and eat." He made a drumming motion with his hands. "Get it. Netflix and Chill."

"I got that," Kat said, even as Briley ushered them out of the house. "I can drive, you know."

"Don't be silly. We'll all go together." Briley climbed into the passenger seat of Leah's Escalade. Kat climbed into the back seat.

She had no problem going out but wouldn't have minded staying at home. The past week was long, and she had a feeling it was going to be an even longer night.

Twenty minutes later, Leah pulled up to the venue and left their car to the valet. Once inside, Kat followed Briley and was cordial when Briley would introduce her to someone new. She scanned the area and sucked in a breath when she spied Dylan at one of the serving tables. Oh, my. She wore a bowtie. What were the odds they would keep running into each other?

"What has your attention?" Leah handed her a glass of cider. "Is that the woman from the Burger Café?"

Kat sipped her drink. "It is."

"Are you going to stare at her like some kind of creep or are you going to go talk to her?" Leah took a sip of her cider.

"Well, Briley creeping on you worked out."

"That's a bit different. I knew Briley was a bit off when she approached me. This woman doesn't know you. Not really."

"I see your point, but she's working. I don't want to get her in trouble."

"Kat, I had hope for you when you took the reins and helped Briley and I get together. But it looks like you're are as hopeless as she was." Leah took the drink out of her hand. "Go."

"Okay." She cleared her throat. "Okay." As she walked across the room, she glimpsed the tulips, then whipped out her phone to research tulip color meanings. Yellow tulips represented happy occasions. She plucked one out of the vase, gave herself an internal pep talk, but felt positive when she stepped up to the table that it had failed. Dylan was beautiful.

"Meatball?"

"Uh…okay." She handed the tulip over. "This is for you."

Dylan accepted it and smiled. "I'm not sure you're supposed to take these from the tables, but I appreciate the gesture."

"Oh." Kat felt only slightly embarrassed, then grabbed a saucer and held it out, Dylan putting two meatballs on it.

"More?"

"What?" Why was this so awkward?

"Do you want more?" Dylan gestured with her fork to the meatballs.

"No thanks." Kat pulled the saucer back and licked her lips. "Dylan, you look pretty tonight."

"That's what I told her when she arrived tonight," Haley threw in.

Kat cut her eyes to the woman standing beside

Dylan. Probably a few years younger than them in a girl next door sort of way. Kind of like Briley. She slowly turned back to Dylan. "It's…yes, well. I should…"

"I guess you should."

"Okay." She turned to leave when Dylan called her name. "Yes?"

Dylan held out a fork. "You're going to need this."

"Yes." Kat made sure to grab the fork low enough that her fingers brushed against Dylan's. "Could I have a dance with you later?"

Dylan paused, then answered. "I would like that…but I'm working."

Crashed and burned. "Of course. Sorry, I don't want to get you in trouble. Have a good night." She turned quickly and practically flew across the room to join Leah and Briley, who were seated at a small table. Kat sat and placed the saucer on the table top.

"The flower was a nice touch." Leah grabbed the fork from her hand and speared a meatball. "But I take it that didn't go well?" She slipped the meatball in her mouth and chewed.

"What a disaster." Before she could eat the other meatball, Briley ate it. "That was mine."

"You weren't going to eat it," Briley said.

"Whatever."

"Kat." Leah touched her hand. "It couldn't have been that bad."

"Well, my speech reverted back to a toddler and I stared at her a lot, probably with my jaw dropped. I can't remember, and, like an idiot, I asked her to dance, knowing she was working. Besides, she might not even be gay."

"Only one way to find out is to ask her," Briley said, then smirked. "An idiot is right; I wasn't even that weird around Leah."

"That doesn't make me feel any better, Bri." She rubbed the back of her neck. "I don't know. Maybe I should forget about her and this tiny crush."

"Tiny crush," Leah said, rolling her eyes.

"More like you can see it from the moon," Briley added.

"You know, you two really know how to make a girl feel good." Kat downed the rest of her cider, then grabbed another one from a passing waiter. "I complimented her looks."

"Now that," Leah said, "is a start."

"All right." Kat held out her hand to Leah. "Would you like to dance?"

Leah placed her hand in Kat's. "I would love to."

※※※※

Dylan pasted on a fake smile at yet another drunk man as she placed two more meatballs on his already full plate. Another fifteen minutes and her night would be over. After the appetizers, everyone would move into the adjoining ballroom where the Mayor and a few people would speak, and the donations would be collected.

More than once, her eyes had sought Kat out and she hadn't been disappointed. Most of the time, Kat danced with Leah and a couple other women and they all seemed to be having a good time. One part of her wished she could dance with Kat and another part was glad she didn't. Her crush was getting a tad bit out of control. The tulip was a nice surprise, though. After their run-in at the nursery the previous week, she had a feeling Kat knew exactly what she was doing when she gave her the yellow tulip and not the pink one.

Having someone interested in her felt nice, but she had so much going on now.

"Hallelujah," Haley said as the last guests walked into the ballroom. "Let's get this stuff into the kitchen so we can clean up then divide the food."

"Sounds good."

Fifty minutes later, the tables were stacked, the food was divided, and the kitchen cleaned. Nobody had wanted the meatballs, so she had two large Styrofoam containers filled that she would be able to divide and freeze for a quick snack for Emma for the next couple of weeks. There were a few beef rolls left and she and another woman split them. They each were given a small container with an assortment of desserts.

"Here," Gayle said, handing her another container. "It's for Emma. I know how much she likes my cream puffs. There weren't many left, but I wanted to make sure she got them."

"She'll love them. Thank you." Dylan slipped the container and the check Haley gave her into her purse. "If you ever need any help, give me a call."

"I will. Have a good night."

"What did she give you?" Haley asked while peeking at her bag.

"The last of the cream puffs." Dylan almost laughed at the look on Haley's face.

"I asked her if there were any left and she said no."

"Well, there weren't any. She gave them to Emma."

They both grabbed their purses and their bags with leftovers. Dylan waved to the other two workers and walked out with Haley. "It's a beautiful night."

"That it is. I could have covered for you if you wanted to dance with Kat."

"While I appreciate the sentiment, I would never do that while I was working."

"I get it." Haley paused. "She likes you."

Dylan shrugged. "I don't know."

"No, Dylan. The way she looked at you said it all. She likes you. That was clear as day. Don't be scared to like her back."

"I'll think about it."

"That's all I ask. You deserve to have someone in your life that's going to look at you like Kat does." At their cars, Haley squeezed Dylan's arm. "That's all I'm going to say on that subject. I'll see you at work on Sunday."

"I'll be there." Dylan unlocked her car and set the bags in the passenger seat then climbed in and started it. She laid the tulip on top of her bag. As she pulled out, she had hoped to get another glimpse of Kat but was glad she was going to be getting home an hour earlier than planned.

She hadn't expected Kat to be so tongue tied and found it endearing. As many times as they'd met, Dylan had a feeling it wasn't the last time she would be seeing her. At least, she hoped it wasn't.

Chapter Eight

Kat crossed her arms and glared at the beast in the field in front of them. Stupid Briley and her stupid ideas. If she knew this is where they were going, she would have never gotten up so early. The previous night she'd kept Griffin, but she'd woken up from a nightmare and insisted on being taken home. Kat had tried to calm her down, so as not to interrupt Briley and Leah's date night, but Griffin wasn't having any of it.

"Kat, really. Why so glum?" Briley asked, while sporting a feral grin.

"I hate you."

"No, you don't."

When Briley had called her this morning and asked if Kat wanted to join them for the day, she'd readily agreed. Her first clue something was up happened when Briley wouldn't tell her where they were going and kept avoiding her eyes. They'd arrived at their destination first, with the promise of Leah, Evan, and Griffin to follow.

"Briley, I don't even like horses." Kat groaned. "You don't like horses." She pointed to the corrals in the distance. "Can Griff even ride?"

"Don't be silly. They're only animals." Briley waved her hand dismissively. "And no, but she'll enjoy being here."

At Briley's tone of voice, Kat turned and looked

at her. Briley projected an air of calm, but Kat had known her long enough to see beyond the exterior and zeroed in on the tenseness of her jaw. "Well, at least we're both in this mess."

"Shut up."

Kat laughed. "What did Leah have to do to get you to agree to this?" They hadn't ridden since the disaster during their vacation to Colorado when they were kids, where they were both thrown from their horses. Briley ended up with a broken wrist and Kat suffered a mild concussion. It was the worst vacation they'd ever been on.

Briley sighed and adjusted her ball cap. "She asked."

"Christ, Briley, you're whipped. Why invite me?"

"Don't be stupid, Kat. Why wouldn't we invite you? You're my sister and we love you."

That made her feel a little better. "Thanks." She placed her arm around Briley's shoulders.

"Besides, there is no way I'm doing this without you. You should be as traumatized as me. It's only fair."

"Figures." Kat turned at the sound of a car pulling up, then focused back on Briley when it wasn't Leah's Escalade. However, she spun back around as a familiar voice came from the direction of the car.

"What is it, Kat?" Briley questioned and turned to look at what she was staring at.

Dylan exited the car, Kat taking in her long hair put up off her neck with a clip and noticed she wore a pair of blue jeans and a white t-shirt with a red, paisley button down top over it.

Kat stopped breathing when Dylan smiled and briefly waved at her. Even from this distance, Kat could make out those cute dimples before Dylan focused her attention on Iris, who exited out the back seat of the car. Once more, Kat turned back to her sister and gestured at the car.

"Fifth time's a charm," Briley said. Apparently, Briley was keeping count. Evan must have filled her in on the encounter at the nursery.

"Don't remind me. I can't believe I chickened out last time. Even Evan has more game than I do."

"Tis true. Go say hi." Briley gave her a nudge, but Kat stood her ground when she spied Leah's SUV pull into the lot. Then her gaze swung to the other car as Dylan opened the passenger side door and helped a small child out. The little girl had a huge smile, but the prosthetic on her right leg held Kat's attention. Dylan bent over and kissed her on the forehead, then nodded at what the little girl was saying.

"Aunt Kat."

Kat barely had time to catch the whirlwind that was Griffin, who hugged her legs tight. Kat feigned nonchalance, then bent down, lifted a squirming Griffin into the air upside down and dangled her until they were face to face. "Hello, monkey." Kat kissed a laughing Griffin's nose, then set her upright on the ground.

"Horses." Griffins small frame vibrated with excitement as she bounced on her feet.

Her excitement was palpable, but Kat still wasn't looking forward to what she'd gotten herself into. "I know. Ready to have some fun?" Griffin bobbed her head then lifted her arms to be picked up.

"She's been clingy since her nightmare last night," Leah said, then kissed Kat on the cheek. Kat slipped her arm around Leah's shoulders, then turned to find the others. She narrowed her eyes when she noticed Briley and Evan were standing beside Dylan, Iris, and the little girl. "Let's go see what they're up to." She squeezed Kat. "It's okay to like her."

Kat licked her lips. "Okay." She didn't know why she was so nervous. The woman was a stranger. Well, by this point, more like an acquaintance. Good grief, she wasn't some nervous person who let her feelings or thoughts get out of control. With each step in their direction, her body felt weighted down. Dylan talked to a tall, rugged man, wearing a cowboy hat. They stopped beside the small group.

"Hello."

Kat looked down at the voice, then smiled. The joy that radiated off the small face instantly made Kat feel lighter. A face that looked exactly like Dylan's, down to the dimples. "Hello."

The little girl held a hand out for Kat. "I'm Emma. Are you going to ride a horse today too?"

Kat held Griffin on her left hip while she took the small hand in a gentle shake. "I'm Kat, and I hadn't planned on it." Kat was aware of the other people's eyes on them both.

"Of course, she is," Briley cut in. "It's a family day."

"What's the matter, Aunt Kat? Are you scared?" Evan said, then did a handstand much to Griffin's delight, who wiggled to be put down. Kat put her back on the ground and watched while she ran into her brother's arms. He threw her in the air and caught her.

Kat pushed her hands in her pockets. "Those are fighting words, Evan. And if you knew the experience Briley and I had when we were younger, you'd understand my reluctance."

"Oh?" Leah slipped off her sunglasses and nibbled

the ear piece as she looked from Kat to Briley. "Does this have to do with Colorado?" She looked again from Briley to Kat, who both wore grim looks on their faces and made the sign of the cross.

"We don't talk about some events of that trip, Leah," Briley said, softly. "At least not in public. I'll tell you later." She adjusted her glasses.

Kat agreed. "Not in public." It always amazed her that with everything Briley had shared with Leah, apparently, Briley never told her about all that happened in Colorado. Kat figured that was about to change.

"You're funny," Emma said.

Kat pivoted then bowed her head toward Emma. "Why thank you, little lady." Emma giggled, and Kat looked up when a hand was thrust in her direction.

"Good to see you again, Kat," Iris said.

"You as well, ma'am." Kat wiped her hand on her pants before taking the elegant older woman's hand. Kat breathed out when Iris took her hand back, then she met with the amused eyes of Dylan. "Dylan, it's good to see you again as well."

Dylan smiled. "You too."

"Mom, you know her?" Emma asked, pointing at Kat.

Dylan pushed the bangs out of Emma's eyes. "We've run into each other a few times."

"You sure you're not going to ride?" Emma asked again. "I mean, I only have one leg but I'm going to ride. Seems kind of silly you're not even going to try."

All the adults grew quiet as Kat regarded Emma and what she'd said. Kat's heart constricted at Emma's words. "You're right, it is kind of silly, isn't it?" Kat grinned at the little girl who was a spitting image of

Dylan. "For you, I'll give it a try."

Emma scrunched her nose. "Why? You don't even know me."

"Maybe not, but sometimes you meet people that give you a different outlook and it changes the way you see things. It would be silly not to give it another try."

"I did that?" Emma placed her hand on Kat's arm.

"You did."

"Neat."

Kat grinned. "I agree. I hope someday I can do that for someone."

"All right, Dylan, Emma, Iris, is everyone ready to get started?" The man Dylan talked to earlier asked.

"We are," Dylan said. "Emma, tell everyone bye."

"We're not riding together?" Emma asked.

"I'm afraid not, sweetheart," Iris said. "You know all your one-on-one sessions with your trainer were scheduled months ago."

"Okay." Emma looked crestfallen. "Bye Kat. It was nice to meet you." Emma waved at her.

"Nice to meet you as well," Kat said, as Iris and Emma walked into the large barn.

Dylan nodded. "That's my daughter. She's seven."

"She's great," Kat said, afraid of saying the wrong thing. She rocked back on her heels and noticed her family had moved away to give them some privacy. "Really, she's great. I like kids." Kat knew she was rambling, something she did when nervous.

"I think so." Dylan pointed behind her. "I should get in there with them."

"Of course, I...one moment." Kat ran a few steps to the left and plucked a dandelion from the ground. She knew the flower represented many things;

the important one for her was surviving through all challenges and difficulties. She jogged back and presented it to Dylan.

Dylan smiled and made sure not to squish the flower. "Thank you." She gestured with a quick tilt of her head toward the stables. "I really need to get in there."

"I understand. We're going for ice cream afterwards if you all wanted to join us." From the look on Dylan's face, she was surprised by the words as Kat was with the invitation. "I mean. If you're not busy. It's cool if you are. Cool. Cool." What was wrong with her?

"For ice cream?"

Kat ran her hand through her hair, which, she knew, stuck up in several places by now. "Yes."

"Are you asking me out on a date…or just going out as friends?"

Kat knew she had to be careful here. She thought it a good idea to take it slow for now and ease into more later. "As friends. You know, get to know you better. I haven't lived in Garriety long and besides my sister, her family and friends, along with my two employees, I don't know a lot of people." She decided to go for it. "I wouldn't be averse to dating later on, depending on how our friendship goes." Jeez, could she crawl out of the hole she dug?

"Truthfully, I'm not looking for a relationship at this moment." Dylan smiled. "But friendship is something I'd be interested in." She paused. "If it's okay, let me get back to you on the ice cream, but right now, I need to focus on Emma. Saturdays are our days together."

"You bet. I don't want to take time away from your daughter." When Dylan turned to walk away, Kat hollered for her to stop. "We should exchange numbers. So, you can tell me if you want to join us for ice cream."

"Sure."

Kat ran the few steps up to her. She accepted Kat's phone and punched in her numbers. When she handed it back, Kat sent her a short text message. "We good now?"

"Yep. Friendship has to start somewhere and what better place than over ice cream." Kat looked over her shoulder then back to Dylan. "I should go back with my family also. It was nice to see you today, and nice meeting Emma and seeing your mom again."

"You too, Kat."

Kat watched her walk away with a lump in her throat. Hearing her name roll off Dylan's lips felt nice. Too nice. She jumped when a hand landed on her shoulder.

"Nice," Evan said. "I didn't think you had it in you."

"Don't be silly. She was being nice, and friendship could be on the table." She smacked his shoulder when he rolled his eyes.

"From experience, a girl usually doesn't give her number away on a whim," Evan said.

"From your own experience?"

"You bet."

"Don't get many numbers, huh?"

He shrugged and guided her toward where everyone else was. "It only takes one."

Kat smiled when she reached Briley and Leah, then took a photo of Griffin with her riding hat on. In the distance, she watched Dylan lean over a fence to speak with Emma who sat astride a horse. Without thinking, she raised her phone, zoomed in, and took a picture of them. After slipping her phone in her pocket, she joined Briley.

"So," Kat said, rubbing her hands together. "Which beast is mine?"

❧❧❧❧

Dylan tried to keep her eyes off the group in the distance but couldn't stop herself. A new friendship was exactly what she needed, but a scary first step to take. She'd honestly expected Kat to make a move far sooner.

"I like her, Dylan," Iris said. "She was good to Emma."

"I know. She gave me a dandelion."

Iris frowned. "A weed."

Dylan laughed. "Not just a weed. She knows I love flowers and appreciates the meanings behind them. The floral meaning of the dandelion is a promise of total faithfulness, but I have a feeling she was going with one of the other meanings. Maybe, a gift to someone that will provide happiness."

Iris glanced toward where Emma was. "That was sweet of her."

"It was."

"And how does that make you feel?"

"Like she's trying but doesn't want to come off too strong."

"I agree."

"She also invited us to join them for ice cream later. When I told her that I wasn't looking for a relationship right now, she suggested we could be friends. She hasn't lived here that long."

"Good. I think she would be good for you. In

whatever capacity that entails. Friends are invaluable. And who can say no to ice cream?"

"So, I should go?" Dylan bit her lip. No way would she take Emma with her. The last thing needed right now was for her daughter to become attached to Kat.

"Why not? You like her. It's plain as day and there is nothing wrong with that. She likes you, and Emma, and Kat seems to enjoy being with her family. Stop overthinking everything. Do you want to have ice cream with them?"

"Yes." At her mom's smile, Dylan rolled her eyes. "Yes, I'm not sure it's a good idea. Too soon."

"Too soon for what? It's just ice cream. You're not dating. You're going to try and be friends. And on the way home we can stop by the store and pick up some ice cream for myself and Emma."

"You're right. It is just ice cream and I could use another friend. It would be nice."

"Yes, it would be nice." Iris patted her hand.

Dylan lifted her phone when it vibrated, and her heart thudded when she saw it was from Kat.

Kat: Your kid is a natural. Maybe I should take lessons from her. It's been so long, I'm not even sure I can get on my horse.

Dylan: You should definitely concentrate on your own horse. Falling off would be a bad idea.

Kat: You don't have to tell me. Once was enough.
Dylan: Colorado?
Kat: (groaning) Colorado.
Dylan: I would love to have ice cream with you.

Dylan looked up when someone hooted and couldn't keep the smile off her face when she noticed Kat high-five Evan. She held back her laugh, but her stomach fluttered at Kat's obvious happiness.

Kat: *Excellent. We were going to Cones and Cream around three. Is that good?*

Dylan: *I'll meet you there.*

A moment later, Dylan received a thumb up emoji. She brought up the video option on her phone, pointed it at Emma and started recording. Times like these, with Emma being so carefree, made up for all the bad times. It made everything worth it. Dylan smiled when Emma laughed.

"You've done good, baby." Iris squeezed Dylan's shoulder.

Dylan saved the video and slipped her phone in her pocket. "You really think so? Sometimes it doesn't feel like enough. I wish there was more money in the bank. Emma deserves so much more than I can give her."

"Just look at that smile. Trust me on this. You've done good. We can't always give our children everything they want, but you give her what she needs and then some. You have a happy little girl."

Her eyes strayed to a running and squealing Griffin, her arms swinging in the air and Briley hot on her heels. For a brief moment, she remembered Emma being that age. Before the accident, Emma was a force to be reckoned with. True, Emma still had that same fire, but it now focused on other things.

"Honey, why the doubts suddenly?"

Her mom must have sensed her mood change to a pensive one. "It's not sudden. When I'm holding her from a nightmare and panic attack, I wonder if it's all enough. Will she resent me when she's older? Will she feel less than the other children?"

"Stop." Iris moved until she stood in front of

Dylan and gripped her shoulders. "Repeat after me."

Dylan rolled her eyes. "Mom, I'm not a kid anymore." Iris held steady. "Fine." How embarrassing.

"Repeat after me," Iris said. "I'm a good mom."

Dylan sighed. "I'm a good mom."

"I'm doing the best I can, and my best is good enough." Dylan repeated after her mom then grabbed her in a fierce hug.

"Thank you for being you."

"Always," Iris said.

"I want a hug," Emma shouted from the horse she was astride, and Dylan climbed up on the fence and carefully embraced her little miracle.

"Guess what?"

"What?"

"You and Grams gets to have ice cream while I go out for a couple of hours this afternoon."

Emma cupped her mom's cheek. "Cookie dough?"

Dylan smiled. "If that's what you want."

"Awesome."

Dylan held Emma steady. "You're okay with me going out for a bit?" She wouldn't do it if Emma said no.

"Of course, Mom," Emma said before being led off for a couple more laps around the corral.

Dylan pulled her hair down, then put it back up. "You know what. It's not a big deal."

"Good."

Dylan glanced back at the other group. Kat and Evan were sword fighting with what looked like large sticks. A smile graced her lips when Griffin joined in and Kat faked a stab wound and fell to the ground while Evan picked up a triumphant Griffin and put her on his shoulders. He placed his foot on Kat's chest and the tip of his sword at her neck. Kat seemed perfect. Too perfect.

Could it all really be this easy? Girl meets girl, and everything falls into place. Life wasn't that simple. At least not for her, but one look at their grinning faces and at Emma's happiness was all the push she needed. If fate wanted her to spend time with Kat and her family, she would. Whether a romantic relationship stemmed from that, she didn't know, but she was willing to take the chance on a friendship and see what happened.

Emma remained her number one priority, but she was willing to make room for someone else, if they were willing to make room for her and Emma. Dylan had a feeling Kat was that type of person, but time would tell. First, though, they had an ice cream trip to get through.

Chapter Nine

Kat, freshly showered, towel wrapped around her waist, stared into her closet, and grimaced at the selection of clothes. Stripes sat calmly by her feet. A quick glance at the clock told her she only had ten minutes until it was time to be at Briley's house to leave for ice cream. She didn't have time to waste. Groaning in frustration, she grabbed the first pair of skinny jeans she saw off the hanger then threw them on the bed. She plucked a gray long sleeve t-shirt out and dressed. She pulled on a pair of tiger striped socks and slipped on a pair of sneakers, picked Stripes up, and headed downstairs.

With a couple of minutes to spare, she gave Stripes a quick cuddle, before putting him back on the couch, locking up, and walking across the street to Briley's house. Leah and Griffin were seated on the porch swing and Briley stared Kat down while pointing at her watch.

"I'm here, aren't I?"

"Barely," Briley threw back at her.

Leah slid into the backseat and buckled Griffin in. Kat would have preferred Leah sit in the passenger seat but took her spot next to Briley.

"Where's Evan?" Kat asked.

"At a friend's house. It's only going to be us girls for ice cream."

"Maybe," Kat said.

"What do you mean maybe?" Briley flicked the

turn signal and took a right on Dublin Street.

"Stop at the flower shop on East Fourth. I don't know if Dylan is bringing anyone besides herself. The way she talked it was only going to be her."

"Don't you have her number?" Briley asked.

"Yes, but I only texted her this morning."

"Kat, I've never known you to be hesitant when it came to liking someone before."

"Bri, it's different this time. She has a child. It changes things."

"But you want kids," Briley insisted.

"I do."

"Briley," Leah piped in from the backseat. "I understand what she's saying. If you hadn't already known Evan when we started dating, I would have waited until I was sure of us before letting you two meet. Kids get attached. No matter their age."

"And she's special needs." Kat shook her head "I can't imagine the extra toll that takes on them. I get tired after only keeping Griff for a couple of days. I don't want to add any stress to her life."

"Then why the invite to begin with?" Briley said as she pulled into the parking lot of Sweet Creations Florist.

Kat narrowed her eyes at Briley. "I sort of blurted it out. Sort of like your proposal."

"I hear that." Briley squeezed Kat's knee. "Let's head in."

Kat stared at Briley. "You don't have to go in with me."

"Don't be silly. I'll get Leah something."

Once inside, Kat knew exactly what she wanted.

"Can I help you with something?" the woman behind the counter asked.

Kat noticed her name tag read Harper. "I need a single yellow rose, Harper. One rose, nothing else."

"All right," Harper said.

"And I'll have a single orange rose," Briley said.

Kat stared at Briley when Harper walked off.

"What?" Briley asked. "You're not the only one that's been looking up flower meanings."

"All right." Kat remembered reading that an orange rose meant desire, passion, and enthusiasm.

Five minutes later, they were on their way. Leah seemed happy with her flower and Kat hoped Dylan would be as well. Would it be weird for Dylan to carry a flower into an ice cream shop? "Shoot."

"What?" Leah touched her shoulder.

Kat turned to look at her. "Is it weird me giving her this flower? Would you be upset about it?"

"Me, no, but I don't know Dylan. Do I think she'll be upset, well, I hope not, but I wouldn't see why she would be."

"Okay. That's good."

When they parked and got out, Kat hung back while Briley, Leah, and Griff walked ahead of her.

"Kat."

Kat stopped and turned to Dylan, who walked toward her in a pink and white shirt, jeans, and a pair of sandals. "You look nice." She felt only a little disappointed Emma and Iris wasn't with her, but she understood. She handed the rose to Dylan. "For you."

Dylan took the rose, lifted it to her nose and sniffed. "Thank you."

Kat fidgeted. "It's not weird? I mean, I hoped giving you a flower wouldn't be, but maybe I'm making it weird." She grimaced. "It's stupid, right?"

Dylan stilled her with a hand on her arm. "It's

not stupid. It's lovely. Thank you."

"Good. Good." Dylan's hand was warm on her arm and her fingers so soft. Kat stuffed her hands in the pocket of her pants to stop herself from tugging Dylan into her arms. "I hope I didn't overstep by asking you for ice cream."

"Kat." Dylan touched her arm. "I wouldn't have accepted if I didn't want to."

"Kat." Kat turned her head at a smiling Briley, who hung half out of the door. "We have a table."

"Okay." Kat turned back around and gestured toward the inside of the shop as she held open the door. "After you."

"How chivalrous."

"I try."

Dylan smiled, and Kat had to admit maybe taking a play out of Briley's book was a good start. They walked in and Kat pointed to a waving Briley in the back corner.

Leah, Griffin, and Briley sat on one side of the table, while Kat and Dylan slid into the other side. Kat held back from sliding in close to her. Best to keep a bit of distance between them.

Kat didn't even bother to look at the menu; she got the same thing every time. A small bowl that consisted of a scoop of cookies 'n' cream and a scoop of cookie dough ice cream, topped with a strawberry drizzle and chopped pecans. Thinking about it made her mouth water.

"Aunt Kat." Griffin held out her hands and made grabby motions, but Leah spoke up.

"No, Griffin. You're going to stay here."

"No, Mommy." Griffin's bottom lip trembled, and Kat stayed quiet to see what Briley or Leah would say. One look from Briley to Griffin and the tears stopped.

Kat was shocked the first time she saw Briley's mom face, but now loved the fact that Briley was a natural.

"Monkey," Kat said. "When we get home, if you want to, you can come over and play with Stripes."

Griffin scrunched up her nose and Kat knew what was coming. "Mittens?"

"Mittens can come too." Mittens was Griffin's kitten.

"Otay."

When Griffin became upset, her words slipped a bit, but Kat was glad the crisis had been averted. She turned to Dylan. "What are you getting?"

"I always get a vanilla milkshake."

"It's a good choice."

After the waitress took their order, Dylan spoke up. "Kat, if you don't mind me asking, how did you get into the tiny house business?"

"I don't mind. I was a CPA and still hold all my licensees and I do some freelance work on the side. You ever feel like something is missing? I felt like that for months before talking with Briley and decided to take a chance. I gave my notice to my firm, sold my condo, and moved here. It was the best decision I've ever made."

"You said firm. Not a one-woman operation?" Dylan asked.

"No." Kat rubbed the back of her neck.

"Kat's modest," Briley threw out. "She was set to make partner with the firm where she worked."

Dylan lifted her brow. "Wow."

"It's wow now, but at the time I was scared to death. Briley is the one to take chances, but this is something I needed." She smiled at the waitress when she gave everyone their orders and winked at Griff before diving in. After a few satisfying bites of ice cream, Kat picked up her phone, accessed the camera, and took several pictures of everyone.

"So good," Briley said, then stuck her spoon into Kat's ice cream and took a large bite.

Kat slapped Briley's hand. "Hey, eat your own, or Leah's."

Briley gave a mock shudder. "Leah got lemon sherbet. Lemon, Kat. I love her, but her taste in cold treats sometimes are questionable. What about you, Dylan, do you have a sweet tooth?"

"I used to have a large one, but it's tamed over the years."

Briley furrowed her brow. "That sucks."

Dylan laughed. "Not when you're trying to lose a few pounds."

"I think you look great," Kat blurted out, then focused on her ice cream when she noticed Leah and Briley's knowing smiles.

"Thank you," Dylan said.

"I agree," Leah said. "You look nice."

Kat sat back while Briley and Dylan discussed their favorite recipes. She had a feeling this crush would be the death of her. At least that's what it felt like. But it could be such a sweet death.

"Kat." Kat turned to Leah. "Have you figured out what you're going as for Halloween this year?" The smug look on her face only meant one thing, trouble. Shit, what did they have planned this year?

That got Dylan's attention. "You dress up for Halloween?"

"Of course." Briley high-fived Leah, then Kat, then dropped her hand when Griffin was too focused on her treat. "We all cosplay."

Kat had to put the skepticism in Dylan's voice

to rest. "Yes. Last year, all three of us went to the toy convention. I was Indiana Jones, Briley, the Eleventh Doctor, and Leah, Captain Marvel."

"For Halloween last year," Leah said, "We all dressed up like the Incredibles."

Kat turned to Dylan. "Leah has her and Evan's costumes done. She's working on Griffin's now, then Briley's. I'm not sure what I'm going as."

"I haven't dressed up since a child," Dylan piped in.

Briley looked offended. "You should join us."

Dylan smiled. "We'll see."

When everyone except Kat and Dylan left to go to the arcade attached to the ice cream shop, Kat's nerves stormed back in full force. It was easy to feel comfortable with Dylan a seat over, but now it was just the two of them. "So?"

Dylan took a sip of her water. "So?"

※ ※ ※ ※

Dylan toyed with her glass of water as she got her thoughts in order. She turned from Kat's penetrating gaze and locked onto the others, who were laughing in the arcade. With only her brief encounter with Kat and her family that morning, Dylan wasn't sure what to expect. She knew they had money, but they weren't snobby at all. They were all so down to earth it had instantly put her at ease. She had to admit she was pleasantly surprised. They were all likable and engaging. Especially Kat.

Dylan could see herself becoming friends with Briley and Leah, but that's not at all how she saw herself with Kat and that scared her. More than she would ever admit. Watching Kat fidget next to her brought a smile to Dylan's lips.

The dandelion that morning, while a nice spur of the moment touch, was different than the yellow rose. Intentional on Kat's part, and one of the nicest things anyone had ever done for her, it filled her with warmth knowing Kat was learning about different flower meanings because of her.

"Thank you for being so good with Emma this morning." That hadn't always been the case with Emma meeting new people. Most saw Emma as a burden and always felt sorry for her and in turn for Dylan. It disgusted her what others thought about their life without even wanting or trying to understand.

Kat looked shocked by Dylan's words. "You don't have to thank me for that. She's a great kid. Maybe we could all do something together sometime?"

Dylan cocked her head. "You seem to mean well, but Emma is my world and her well-being is the only thing that matters to me. So, I would like to hold off on you two spending any time together."

"I would never—"

"Maybe not," Dylan interrupted, "but I really don't know you and," she paused, "Emma gets attached to people quickly. She's been disappointed in the past with people showing up and not sticking around."

"I understand that. I'm not even going to insult you by guessing at how hectic your life is and I mean no disrespect when I say this. I can hardly keep up with Griffin or even Evan when we spend time together, so I can't imagine how busy your life is."

It was refreshing for someone to be so truthful with her. "It is busy and yes, her being disabled is a huge factor in that. It gets hard, but my mother has been my rock and if we didn't live with her, I don't know what we would do."

"Family is so important. I missed Briley when we were apart, but moving here has changed my whole outlook, especially with her having kids now. I don't want to miss a moment of it."

"It was hard when Emma wasn't in school, but now I don't feel so bad when I'm at work, because I'm always there to pick her up."

Kat leaned back in her chair. "Do you mind if I ask what happened?"

Dylan sighed, trying to find the words.

"If it's too much." Kat placed her hand over Dylan's.

"No." Dylan slipped her hand out from underneath Kat's and didn't miss the hurt in Kat's eyes, but it disappeared in a flash. "I don't mind telling you, but not here."

"All right."

"Really?"

Kat grinned. "It means we can spend more time together."

"You have a way with words."

"Trust me, I can be a mess at times, but I try and see the positive outlook on life. Try not to be negative or sad."

"Doesn't that get tiring?" It would wear her out.

"Not really. I think I'm naturally an optimistic go getter."

"You go after what you want."

"Most of the time, but usually not in my relationships. I always seem to hit a roadblock with women."

"I find that hard to believe."

"It's true. The whole time I was helping Briley

overcome her fear and take a chance on Leah, I wished I could be like that. It's not a problem meeting women, but finding that balance between a relationship, family, and my work can be a tough pill to swallow. From watching and talking with both Briley and Leah, I know what it takes to make a successful romantic relationship work and it's a lot. Throw in kids and that's twice the pressure not to screw anything up."

"That's the most refreshing and honest thing I think anyone has ever said to me. Thank you for your honesty. If I'm also being honest, I would love to be in a relationship; it gets lonely sometimes, but I don't have the extra time to devote to the work it would take either. I know friendship takes work, but it's something I'm willing to try with you. I genuinely like you and so does Emma. I don't have a lot of free time, but you're welcome to join us on some of our excursions after we get to know each other a little. I'm also not opposed to texting or talking at night." She wasn't sure where her bout of courage came from, but she wasn't about to question it.

"That's..." Kat ran her fingers through her hair, "great. I would really like that. I don't have a lot of extra time either, but I can make time for you and Emma in the future. I have standing dates with Griffin and Briley once a week, and Evan and Leah once a month, but besides that, I'm yours."

Dylan knew what she wanted to say but didn't want to stray beyond friendship right now. "Sounds good."

"So," Kat said.

"We have plans to go to the zoo this coming Saturday, but I can meet you after for maybe an hour. I try to spend my days off with Emma."

"I would like that. I can't even count how many times I've been to the zoo with Griffin since I moved here. And I don't want to take time away from you and Emma."

"I can spare an hour. Meet me at Brew and Bake at two."

"I'll be there." Kat smiled shyly. "It's all right to text?"

"Yes. That's all right."

"Okay." Kat stood and offered her hand to Dylan, who took it and enjoyed the feel of Kat's hand in hers. "Let's join the others." She puffed up. "I don't want to brag, but I'm good at arcade games."

Dylan arched her brow. "If you didn't want to brag, you wouldn't have said anything. But I do believe I can give you a run for your money."

"Maybe, maybe not. You have to watch us Anderson women. We do like winning. Briley more than me."

"Is that right?"

Kat leaned near and Dylan's heart thudded hard at the closeness. God, she smelled good. "I'll let you in on a secret. I have, in the past, let Briley win because I know she's a sore loser. Don't tell her I said that, though, she'd flip, but she is my little sister."

"Your secrets are safe with me."

"I had a feeling they would be."

Kat led her through the crowd and into the arcade. They quickly located the others, but Kat didn't let go of her hand until Griffin noticed her and demanded to be picked up. Dylan felt it was going to be far easier than either one of them expected to find the time to spend together. Surprisingly that wasn't as scary as she thought it would be.

Chapter Ten

Kat hummed as her feet pounded the pavement, Briley keeping up pace beside her. They were on their last mile, and she could tell Briley was starting to feel it. "You doing okay, Bri?" She ignored the glare Briley shot at her and grinned.

"I...yes." She huffed. "I'm good. I don't normally run this many miles."

"It's good for you. We're almost there." Ten minutes later, Kat stood over a sprawled-out Briley, who had flopped onto the ground with a growl the moment they reached Kat's yard. She pushed her foot up against Briley's side. "Don't growl at me."

"That sucked."

"Don't be such a baby. Keeping in shape is good for you."

"I know." Briley held her hand out and Kat grasped it and hauled her to her feet. "Next time I'll do better."

Kat patted her back. "That's the spirit."

Briley accepted the water Kat offered and downed half of it. "So, Dylan?"

"What about her?"

"You like her. Don't lie. I can tell."

"I do like her, but neither one of us has time for dating, but we've agreed to try and be friends."

Briley frowned. "You're okay with that?"

"I am. They're going to the zoo today, but

afterward, Dylan and I are going to have coffee."

"Good for you." Briley smirked.

Kat rolled her eyes. "Yes. I figured it's time I made friends outside of your friends."

"I think it's great. Have fun today."

"You too." Kat fell back against the door when she shut it behind her. She'd never admit it to Briley, but that last mile had gotten to her. The only reason she added it on was to grate on Briley and it had almost backfired.

It was only seven, and she wasn't supposed to meet Dylan until two. Plenty of time yet. After a leisurely shower, she fixed an egg white omelet, then settled down on the couch to watch some TV She smiled when she caught sight of Stripes crawling onto the couch, dressed in a red and white hoodie. Briley must have dressed him before they left for their run. He settled around her neck.

"I'm going somewhere today, Stripes, but I'll play with you tonight, buddy. I've been busy, and I've made a few new friends. I think you'll like Emma. I've only met her once, but she seemed great." Earlier, he'd eaten his breakfast of lamb hearts before she'd went for a run, so he was content with a quick cuddle. Before she left for the coffee shop, she would give him some minced beef to hold him over until Briley swung by to feed him later. He was a good companion and she was glad she'd added him to her family. He was free to roam during the day, but at night he preferred to sleep in her office in his hammock. She'd tried having him sleep with her, but his constant nipping kept waking her up. She wasn't high maintenance, but she did enjoy a full eight hours of uninterrupted sleep.

Just as she finished drying her plate, a text

message arrived. Her smile dropped when she read it.

Dylan: *Not going to the zoo today. Emma had a bad night.*

Kat: *I understand. If you need anything, let me know.*

A few minutes later she received another text.

Dylan: *I can still make it at two. Emma insisted.*

Kat: *Only if you're sure?*

Dylan: *I am.*

Kat: *I can't wait.*

Dylan: *Okay. See you at two.*

Kat: *I'll be there.*

Kat sighed and slid down to sit on the kitchen floor and smiled when Stripes raced toward her. She wasn't sure what a bad night entailed for Emma, but it couldn't be anything good. It was eight and if she stayed home, she'd be bored out of her mind. Today was a rare Saturday that she didn't have to do anything for work. Scooping Stripes up, she got to her feet. "How about we visit Griffin today?" After what she was sure was a nod from Stripes, she slipped his harness on, then clipped the leash to it.

The walk across the street was quick and, not five minutes later, she pulled open the backdoor of Briley's house, walked in, and unclipped Stripes so he could run around.

Leah turned from the sink. "Didn't expect to see you this morning."

Kat picked up a towel, helping her dry. "Zoo was cancelled. Emma had a bad night, but Dylan said we're still on for two. So, I thought I would see what you losers were up to and spend the day here."

Leah smirked. "Briley and Griffin aren't here."

"Oh." She thought maybe Evan had taken the

truck when she didn't see it in the drive.

"They left a few minutes ago but will be back soon. Something about a surprise."

"Briley and her surprises. Now she's recruiting the kids to help."

"Not all the kids," Evan said, walking in. "She had this certain gleam in her eye, and I was sure I did not want to be a part of whatever she had in mind."

"A gleam." Leah sighed. "That's not good." She leaned back against the counter. "Did she say anything else?"

He held his hands up. "No. Well, she was bouncing around a bit and being giggly."

Kat shared a look with Leah. That was a bad sign. "It's too late to do anything about it now."

"God help us," Leah threw in.

"Evan, what are your plans for today?" Kat asked, while he bent down to pick up Stripes.

"Nothing really. Just spending the day at home. It's one of those days, you know?"

She did know. All too well. The last year pressed hard on him, after his mom and step-mom were killed in a car accident. "So, how about I kick your ass at Mario Kart, then?"

"How is that supposed to make me feel better?"

"Family time."

"I guess."

"Get it ready. I'll be down there in a minute."

"All right." He kissed Leah on the cheek then walked out.

Leah smiled sadly. "He's been up for a while. Sometimes it doesn't feel like I do enough."

"Leah." Kat pulled her into her arms and rested her chin on the top of Leah's head. "You do so much.

It's cliché, but it does take time. He's adjusted well, and he continues to do so. If he ever stopped being the Evan we know, then it would be time to worry, but now, he's still grieving."

Leah squeezed her waist then stepped back, wiping her eyes. "You Anderson women always know the right thing to say."

"We try."

"You do more than try. I am so glad you and Briley came into our lives."

"Me too. I'm going to head down if you need us."

"Try not to throw the controller this time."

"I make no promises."

Leah's laugh followed her out of the kitchen. She headed to the basement apartment where Evan had moved after his moms' accident to give him a sense of freedom. The scene that greeted her was the cutest thing she'd ever seen. Evan was seated on the couch, with Jackson, his Yorkie, curled up on his left side, Mittens sprawled across his lap, and Stripes curled around his neck, watching the T.V. screen. She lifted her phone and snapped a photo before settling beside him on the couch.

He didn't seem fazed in the bit by the animals when he handed her the other controller. Sometimes a cuddle was the best medicine.

"I hope you're ready to lose," Evan said.

"Bring. It. On."

Three hours later, Kat and Evan looked at each other when they heard the truck pull into the driveway. Wordlessly, they both turned off the game and headed for the door. All three pets were curled up in the corner of the room in Jackson's bed, fast asleep. Evan led the way out of the apartment door, making sure to shut it behind them, and they both creeped around the corner of the house.

Briley was grinning at a stoic Leah and gesturing to the truck, where large pieces of Christmas decorations packed the bed. "Shit," Kat said quietly.

"I'm telling you, Aunt Kat, she's been a bit off since you almost beat her in the Christmas decorating competition last year," Evan said. "It's like not everything is firing up there." He tapped his right temple. "Sometimes I'll come upstairs at night, she'll be at the kitchen table scribbling stuff down, when she catches sight of me, she would look so pleased with herself. It was cute and creepy at the same time. One time, Mom caught her, and kissed her on the cheek, then walked out of the room."

She rested her head on Evan's back and tried not to giggle. "She's crazy."

"True, but she's our crazy."

"You're right. Let's go see what she's got, then I'm going to have to head out."

Briley was crazy about decorating for Christmas, and now that she'd moved in with Leah, Kat knew she didn't stand a chance at winning the Christmas decorating competition, but she'd have fun making Briley sweat.

"Sounds good to me. I can watch Stripes for you."

"Sure. His minced beef is in the fridge." She was glad she could be there for Evan but was looking forward to her coffee with Dylan.

Chapter Eleven

Dylan took a deep breath before pushing open the door and entering Brew and Bake. Emma had insisted that she meet with Kat and that she'd be fine. With a nervous wipe of her palms on her pants, she scanned the area, stopping when she saw Kat wave.

What was she doing? This was crazy and absurd, so why did it feel so right? Things were complicated, and they hadn't even started yet.

Kat stood and waited until Dylan sat before she retook her seat. "I'm glad you could make it."

"I almost didn't, but Emma practically shoved me out the door."

"I'm glad. What do you want? I'll get it."

Dylan sat and watched Kat approach the counter and banter with the employee. She always seemed so at ease around people. She wished she could harvest some of Kat's energy. A few minutes later, Kat was back, depositing their drinks and two muffins on the table.

"Here's your banana muffin."

"Thank you."

"My lady." Kat slid the muffin toward her. "So, let's start off with some easy friend questions. Do you have a hobby?"

"I knit."

"Why knitting?" Kat asked.

This she could do. "It relaxes me. I try and make

a new scarf for everyone for Christmas."

"Everyone needs a hobby."

"What do you do for fun?"

"I like to exercise. To relax, I do yoga and meditate. For fun, my sister and I cosplay and go to conventions. I collect superhero figurines and comic books."

"You might have more in common with my daughter than me." It was a sobering fact. She wasn't into any of those things.

"Don't sell yourself short. We don't have to like the same things to be friends."

"I know, but it doesn't hurt."

"Now, we can't let our likes and dislikes divide us before this is even started." Kat gestured to a bookshelf on the far wall of the cafe. "What's your favorite book?"

Dylan relaxed as they discussed different genres and the different authors they liked. Being with Kat was easy and scary at the same time. Kat made her feel so comfortable.

After a lull in conversation, Dylan knew it was time to talk about Emma. "When I found out I was pregnant, I was scared. Ian and I hadn't been married that long, but he was excited. He was a fantastic dad."

"You don't have to…"

Dylan held her hand up. "I don't mind. Emma was our entire life from the moment we found out about her. Ian and I had a solid relationship and baby made three. Emma was two. We had run out of milk and Ian was going to the grocery store to pick some up and a few more items. Emma threw a fit to go with him. I don't remember how long after they left when the first phone call came. Looking back, it seemed close to three hours. I didn't have any reason to worry, though, he would never intentionally let anything happen to her." She shook her head. "We buried Ian on a Thursday, and straight from there I went back to the hospital where Emma was scheduled for another surgery. Over the years, she's had six." Dylan remained still when Kat picked up and cradled Dylan's hand within hers.

"You don't have to go on."

"I don't mind." She squeezed Kat's hand, but held tight. "Her right leg was so mangled the doctors said they could try and save it, but Emma's way of life would be better if it was amputated. She was a champ from the moment she woke up. She gets frustrated a lot but knows how lucky she is to be alive. It's been tough, but I thank God every day that my baby lived."

"I can't even imagine going through that." Kat shook her head and squeezed Dylan's hand.

"She was two, Kat. The bed swallowed her, and there were so many tubes. I don't know how I would have made it if something had happened to her too." She hoped she never felt that kind of pain again.

Kat's expression was somber, her eyes reflecting compassion. "I don't know if I would have been able to survive that."

"It's not something I would wish on my worst enemy. We've come a long way, Emma and I." She closed her eyes, then opened them and stared straight into Kat's. "I've felt guilty over the years because even though I loved Ian, I knew he wasn't my forever. I can't even say if we would still be together now, if he had lived. Looking back, I wonder if I held him back from finding his forever, but I've let that go. I know he loved me, but Emma was his entire life. I have never seen a man so excited and glowing when he found out about her."

"That's awesome. I had a wonderful dad, so I know what that's like, but not everyone does. That he loved her that much tells you what kind of man he was. Also, you shouldn't feel guilty for your feelings. If he was here now, you may not be together, but you would both still be raising an amazing girl. No one knows what the future holds. Briley, once she sorted her feelings for Leah out, there was no stopping her. She went for it and Leah couldn't help but fall for her charms. My point being is that sometimes your once in a lifetime isn't who you think it is, or where you think it should be."

Dylan pulled her hand from Kat's, thinking a change of subject was needed, and there was a matter she needed to make clear. "So, I'm sure you have an idea, or maybe you don't, but I wanted to confirm that I am bisexual. I don't know if that bothers you, but I hope it doesn't."

"No, it doesn't, but thank you for telling me. I wanted to ask but didn't want to sound pushy or nosy."

"If you never ask the question, you'll never get the answer." Dylan took a sip of her water. "Anything to get off your chest, since I unloaded on you?" She wasn't used to opening up to a woman she barely knew. This got heavier than she expected for a first non-coffee date.

"That's what friends are for," Kat said. "Let's see. I'm terrified my business is going to fail. Accounting is something I'm good at. I do enjoy it, but it was so unfulfilling. Tiny houses fascinate me. I like to have a bit more room than that, but for a lot of people they're the right choice."

"Aren't they a jazzed-up camper?"

Kat feigned looking offended. "No. At least I don't think so. It's more like a home, even though you can move it around. A camper, to me, always screams temporary or vacation, but a tiny home is just that. A home. Campers are nice, but if I was choosing one, I would go with a tiny house."

"I've watched some of the shows on TV and some are expensive. The prices are comparable to buying a house."

"Some are, but we do a lot of our stuff in-house. I have two employees. Reeva is a licensed plumber, and Kyle has a knack for building custom cabinets and inserts. The only thing I have to contract out for is the electrical and I'm working on my certification for that right now. We've completed a handful of tiny houses, ranging from twenty-five to seventy-five thousand. The more high-end someone wants it the higher the cost, but we worked with all our clients to give them all that they can for the money they have. A lot of people want that freedom to travel around with their home and not worry about a mortgage or the added cost of want entails with owning a house."

That made complete sense. "I get that. I've thought about buying a camper, so Emma and I can go on vacation. She enjoys camping and fishing, but I wouldn't even know where to start."

"I would be happy to help you look for a camper and if you want, we could work on it together."

"Together?"

Kat fidgeted, but soon gained her confidence. "Me, you for now, maybe Emma in the future. A group project?"

"I would like that, but I don't have the extra money to spend on something like that. Emma's needs are more important right now." Maybe she should tell Kat she was super poor. She took a deep breath.

Kat held her hand up. "I'm not going to charge you for helping work on a camper. We have tons of left over or extra supplies. Most of that stuff can't be used for new builds, but for something like your project, it would be ideal."

"You would just give it to us?" At every turn, Kat kept surprising her. Who was this woman? No one was this nice, were they?

"With a lot of the scraps from our last two builds, Briley and I took the wood and built a treehouse for Griffin. It's kickass if I do say so myself. Evan, I think, enjoys it more than Griff."

"They're your family," Dylan said.

"You're my friend. Look, I'm not trying to be weird or creepy. Think about it. I don't mind helping you. Hell, Evan's even helped from time to time. So, that would be an extra hand."

Was it all really that easy? Dylan didn't think so, but Kat looked so sincere that Dylan didn't have the heart to turn her down, but at the same time, she wouldn't hold her to it. They'd both said they didn't have the extra time for a relationship; how would they have the time to work on a camper? Instead of speaking with her head, she listened to her heart, and raised her water glass. Kat followed suit and clinked them together. "To friendship."

"To friendship," Kat repeated.

Chapter Twelve

While waiting for Kat to arrive, Dylan steeled her nerves. Almost a week had passed since their last face to face and they'd agreed to meet on Thursdays for lunch, since that was Dylan's day off and Kat could get away from her business easy enough.

It was too soon for Emma to spend any time with Kat, but Emma was excited Dylan had made a new friend. She'd wait until she got to know Kat a little more before she allowed her to spend any time with her daughter.

So far, what she'd learned about Kat she liked, but they really didn't know each other, and Dylan hoped she'd be able to put her preconceived notions about friendship to the side and enjoy her time with Kat.

The breeze that washed over her was cool but refreshing.

"Dylan."

Dylan turned her head and stared as Kat walked up. No matter what the other woman chose to wear, she always looked good. Today her hair was spiked on the top of her head, giving her a mini faux hawk. If she had to guess, the hair on top of Kat's head was an inch and a half tall. That, combined with her torn jeans and sleeveless black t-shirt, gave her an air of badassery that for anyone else would be hard to pull off. But, Kat did with ease and Dylan had a feeling it wasn't on purpose.

"Kat." Dylan stood and noticed the flower in Kat's hand. Dylan held back her gasp. It was a pink with yellow center alstroemeria. It was gorgeous and meant friendship and was her favorite flower, but Kat couldn't have known that.

Kat gave a nervous nip to her bottom lip. "This is for you."

"It's beautiful." Dylan held the stem loosely. "Thank you." She walked beside Kat to a food truck that was always set up by the park. "You had no way of knowing but this," she lifted the flower, "is my favorite."

"Really?" Kat looked relieved but pleased with her choice.

"Yes."

Kat slipped her hands in her pockets. "I'll remember that."

"I'm sure you will." One thing she was positive about Kat was that she really listened and didn't put on a front.

"Here," Kat said. "Why don't you sit, and I'll get our food?"

Dylan relayed her order then took a seat at an empty table. She was aware of all the eyes on Kat because hers were as well. She lifted her phone and took a picture of Kat walking away. That wasn't too creepy, she decided. Fifteen minutes later, Kat was headed back with their food. It was a good thing they'd decided to eat at eleven, as to miss the lunch rush.

"Loaded fries, my lady." Kat set down a basket of French fries covered in beef gravy, sharp cheddar cheese cubes, mushrooms, and broccoli. Kat had opted for the fries smothered in white gravy, grilled chicken pieces, and deep-fried green beans. "This food truck is awesome. It was one of the first places that Briley brought me when I moved here."

"Emma enjoys it too." Dylan sprinkled pepper on her food.

"We'll have to bring her sometime." Kat stopped with the fork halfway to her mouth. "That is, if it's okay with you in the future."

"In time." It was refreshing that Kat wanted to get to know Emma. In Dylan's previous dating experiences, most people didn't want an instant family.

Kat lifted her fork and waited for Dylan to do the same. "In time."

They sat side by side and finished their lunch in silence. Dylan pushed her empty basket away and after a sip of water turned to face Kat. "Busy morning?" She figured it was a safe question.

"Yes and no. Nothing I can't handle. How about you?" Kat gathered their trash into a pile.

"It's been an easy morning."

Kat drummed her fingers on the picnic table. "You never said what it is you do for a living."

"I work at a hotel." She knew it wasn't anything prestigious, but it was honest work and paid the bills.

"Do you like it?"

Kat didn't look put off, just interested, so Dylan took her lead and relaxed. "It's a job." Dylan shrugged. "Pays the bills."

"I understand that. That's how I feel about being an accountant. It pays the bills, but I love building the tiny houses."

Dylan suddenly felt way out of her league and couldn't help her nervous fidget. Those weren't the same things at all. She and Kat came from two different worlds. "I…"

Kat fumbled with her water bottle; her expression appeared worried. "What is it? Did I say something wrong?"

"No. No. Look, Kat. Maybe this friendship isn't going to work." Maybe she'd jumped in with both feet way too fast.

"What? Why?"

"You being an accountant and me being a housekeeper are at two ends of a spectrum. Yes, I went to college, but a business degree didn't get me far. I'm not ashamed of my job, and it's just as needed as yours is, but I'm not immune to the fact that they're not even in the same league. I mean, you own your own business." Dylan shook her head. What was she thinking agreeing to this? On the other hand, Kat didn't need her insecurities laid bare. This was their second friend date. "I'm sorry."

Kat frowned. "For what?"

"Unloading on you. You don't deserve that." She squeezed the bridge of her nose. "I'm just…you know or maybe you don't. Sometimes it feels like everything piles in on you. Every day I think about what Emma needs and what I can't afford for her. It gets so frustrating. I'm so thankful for all the organizations that have helped Emma be more independent, but, at the same time, I wish I could have afforded those things for her." She glanced at Kat, who looked anything but bothered by her words.

"You know I'm not rich, right?" Kat tore at the label on her water bottle. "Yes, I've invested well, but I'm also in debt. The business wasn't cheap. I would never think different of you for not having money or the things you don't have. I'm not like that and I hope I haven't come across that way."

"No." Dylan placed her hand on Kat's arm. "No, you haven't. I'm sorry again. I try to get Emma most things she wants, but I can't give her what she needs. It always feels like it's never enough."

Kat straddled the bench and gave her complete attention to Dylan. "Like what? I have time. Lay it on me. I won't judge you, Dylan." She tugged her earlobe. "I'm all ears. This is what friends do."

Dylan laughed but mirrored Kat's position. Maybe not knowing Kat that long was the type of friend she needed to listen to her. "She wants a pet, and while we could go to the shelter, I try to make her realize pets aren't cheap and we can't afford one right now. At one point, she thought a mobility assist dog would be good, but good lord those are so expensive. Who has twenty thousand dollars for a dog?" Kat's eyes widened and her mouth dropped open a little. "Exactly. I didn't realize they were that high either, but with her disability they're expensive. Though, in time, she's realized she doesn't necessarily need one. She gets along so well with her prosthetic, but the time's coming where she's going to need a new one and I know the organizations will help her, but sometimes I see these other families and they have less than we do, and I feel like we're taking something away from them."

"Are the prosthetics expensive?" Kat prodded her.

"If I was to get her another one now, by the time she's fully grown, I would have spent nearly a hundred thousand dollars." Kat whistled. "That's why I'm so thankful for all the non-profits that have helped us. I still have close to a hundred thousand to pay in medical bills." This was not how she had expected lunch to go. No wonder she didn't have many friends.

"Look at me." Kat gripped her hands. "She's happy and healthy. You have nothing to be ashamed about. No, you can't give her those things, but you love her and that's so evident. You've done what you could by reaching out to people that can help her and I'm sure it couldn't have been an easy thing to do. You're trying and that's more than can be said for a lot of parents."

She squeezed Kat's hand. "When I found out how expensive everything was, I felt like I was letting her down. Ian would have known what to do and I… faltered. If it wasn't for my mom, I don't know what I would have done. My dad's wonderful, but he lives seven hours away and Mom's right there." Dylan shook her head but kept a tight grip on Kat's hand. "And the looks I get when people find out I'm on government assistance…" She held Kat's eyes. "There's always judgement. I should work harder, or get more jobs, and so forth."

"Listen to me, Dylan," Kat tilted Dylan's chin up, "I don't care about those things. You're doing what you must do to survive. There is nothing to be ashamed of and I've never understood why people on government assistance are always made to feel less than. At some point in all our lives, we need help. Bless the people or organizations that are there to help us."

Dylan slipped her hand out of Kat's impossibly warm one. "A lot of people don't feel that way."

Kat's smile was sad. "When my dad died, all three of us grieved in our own way. Briley is a crier. Mom locked herself away, and me, well, I bottled everything up inside. A few days after the funeral, my mom and I had a huge fight and I stormed out of the house. When I finally came to my senses, I was a couple of miles from home. I walked without a purpose and ended up across town." She shook her head. "When I realized where I was, I realized I had left my wallet and phone at home. No doubt Briley had tried calling. Later I found out she and Mom had looked for me for hours."

"How'd you get home?"

"I decided to walk through the park and came upon a nursing home outing. Before I could leave, an old man, who later introduced himself as Paul Jones, waved me over to his table where a checker board was set up. We played for an hour. Just played. He didn't mention my tears and I didn't mention him losing." Kat laughed. "When they were ready to leave, one of the nursing home workers agreed to take me home. For the next few months, I joined him at the park. He helped me grieve in my own way. I never really talked with my family over Dad's death. Briley can be persistent, but she loves me and respects my choices. When Paul died, Briley insisted on going to his funeral with me." Kat smiled. "The point of my story is that Paul helped me. If not for him, I don't know where I would be. Sometimes we get help from the most unexpected places and people."

Dylan wasn't ready to delve into her depression after Ian's death. "Do you mind if I ask about your mom?" She needed to take the conversation off herself.

"She still locks herself away. I haven't seen her in two years. We talk, but it's not the same."

"I can't imagine. My mom is my rock."

"Briley is mine. I think that sometimes the right people come into our lives at the right times."

"Fate, Kat?" Dylan scrunched her nose up. "I didn't take you for a fate woman."

"Hey, I believe in fate. I'm not religious, but fate

is something else entirely."

"Are you a romantic, Kat?" She saw it in everything Kat did for her.

Kat reached forward and held both of Dylan's hands. "You better believe I am."

Dylan couldn't take her eyes off her, but the moment was broken when the alarm on Kat's phone went off.

"That's my cue." Kat lifted both of Dylan's hands and kissed them. "I've had a nice time. Can we do this again?"

Dylan laughed. "It was kind of depressing, Kat."

"Pfft, what?" Kat stood then helped Dylan to her feet. "Not depressing, just real. I'm not bothered by your job and I'm proud to spend time with you, but I don't want to push you."

"You're not pushing. I'll see you next Thursday."

"I wouldn't miss it."

With a final wave, Kat walked off. Dylan's eyes stayed glued to her until she was out of sight. For the first time in a long time, Dylan was looking forward to getting to know someone. She had a feeling Kat would make the process interesting.

Chapter Thirteen

Wednesday evening found Kat chopping onions for dinner in the kitchen at Leah and Briley's house. Her thoughts never strayed far from Dylan since their lunch date last Thursday. Saturday she'd worked up the nerve to text Dylan and felt a deep sense of relief when Dylan replied. Every day they'd been texting like clockwork and she'd even received several silly texts from Emma.

All the signs she'd received thus far pointed to the fact that she was going to have to take it slow with Dylan. The last thing she wanted to do was scare her off or push too far. The slower pace didn't bother her, but she hoped that in the end they could move from friendship into more. That was what she wanted to come of this, but she would have to find a way to deal with everything if Dylan ever only wanted to be her friend.

"Something on your mind, Kat?" Leah asked, taking the bowl of chopped onions from her and adding them to the garlic in the skillet.

Kat bit her lip and leaned back against the countertop, sipping from her glass of water. "Can I ask you something?"

Leah stirred the onions. "You don't have to ask if you can ask. Just ask." Leah popped a cherry tomato into her mouth and gave Kat her full attention.

"Okay." Kat's tone was serious. "I know you love

my sister, but Briley can be a little much sometimes. She's fun. With the baking and the dressing up and the Christmas decorating." She lifted her eyebrows. "Did you ever hesitate to date her because some people might see her as too much of a kid? I know most people love her, but there are a few that think she should grow up. That she wasn't enough of a grown up for you."

Leah added the ground beef to the onions, then added all the spices for tacos, before turning back to Kat. "It never bothered me. You know I cosplay with Evan. I guess that is partly the reason I fell in love with her. She is so carefree and alive. At first, I thought the age difference was something I couldn't overcome, but I never saw her as a child. She lives, Kat, and I wouldn't want her any other way."

That was what Kat expected her to say. Leah was fiercely protective of Briley and Kat felt sorry for anyone that dared to put Briley down in front of Leah. "What if she was poor, or at least living paycheck to paycheck?"

Leah turned the burner down, then focused on Kat. "What's bringing this on? I would love Briley no matter what."

"As you know Dylan and I had lunch on Thursday."

"Go on."

"She told me some things and I could tell she was really bothered by them. I wasn't, but I don't want her to ever think I see her differently because," she paused, "because she isn't as well off as I am. I'm not rich, but I'm aware that I have more money in the bank then the average person. I don't have to worry about money, or food, or anything. I can't imagine being stressed because the money isn't there." It hurt her to know how much Dylan was struggling. She and Emma deserved only the best.

"I see." Leah picked up her glass of wine off the countertop and took a sip. "I'm going to assume that Dylan doesn't have a lot of money. I know you, Kat, and you would never discriminate against anyone that's different from you. I get it. I didn't always have money growing up. It's not easy. My mother was always worried. My parents fought. It is stressful, and I know Dylan has a daughter. I can imagine with Emma's disability that is also added stress. It is different for people that have never wanted or never went hungry. I know Briley and I are well off. My children will never want for anything, but part of that is due to the inheritance I got from my father. You need to make sure she knows that you aren't bothered by it."

"Hmmm." Kat nodded and downed the rest of her water. "Did you know a support dog is twenty thousand dollars?"

"I did. I wrote a story about it a few years ago. They are amazing creatures, but not everyone that needs one gets one. Though, there are some grants available and help is out here, but you have to know where to look." Leah turned off the heat to the stove. "Do you want me to gather the information I have? Some things will have changed, but it shouldn't take long to find the updated information.

"No." Kat waved her words off. "Dylan said Emma doesn't need one and she's gotten grants for all her other needs, but you're great for being willing to do so." Kat pulled her into a hug.

Leah chuckled. "I agree, I am."

"She is," Briley said. The two broke apart, but Kat kept her arm around Leah's shoulders.

Briley narrowed her eyes and crossed her arms.

"Planting a stake in my territory, Kat?"

Evan stepped up behind her, holding Griffin, then slipped around Briley. "I'm hungry. Your jealousy can wait, Bri."

"I'm not jealous. Leah is wearing my ring after all." Briley's frown quickly turned into a smile and she bounded across the room and pulled Leah away from Kat. "She knows where her bread is buttered."

"That she does," Kat said, then winked at Leah, who rolled her eyes.

Griffin slapped her hand on the table. "I'm hungry," she whined.

Leah set her shoulders. "Watch the sass." Griffin frowned but kept her mouth shut. "Since you're the breadwinner, Briley, set the table."

Briley laughed, but did what she was told. Yes, this was what Kat wanted.

By nine, Kat was home and putting the final touches on her home office. She'd finally put up the shelves she'd bought weeks ago to hold all her Harley Quinn figurines. Her figure signed by Margot Robbie was one of her most prized in her collection.

Her comics were stored in boxes on floor to ceiling shelves on the back wall. On the wall beside her desk was a Supergirl logo poster signed by every actress that had played Supergirl. From Helen Slater, Laure Vandervoort, and Melissa Benoist, to Joanne Spracklen, who voiced Supergirl in Justice League Action. On the opposite side was a cast signed Batman Beyond poster she'd won in a contest when she was in her early twenties. Her collection of Funko Pops were on shelves that ran seven inches from the ceiling around the room. If she had to choose, this would be her favorite room in her house. It was also one of the biggest.

She had barely finished hanging a cardboard Death Star when her phone vibrated on the desk. The caller brought a smile to her face.

"Dylan, what can I do for you this evening?"

"Emma's in bed and for once, I'm bored. Television wasn't appealing, and neither was knitting."

"Well then, you called the right person. I'm only slightly bored."

"I hope I'm not bothering you."

"You're never a bother. I was organizing my office."

"Sounds dull."

Kat chuckled. "Far from it. This is where I keep all my collectables and comics."

"You did mention you cosplayed."

"I do. It's fun. Gives you a bit of time to be someone different. A superhero, Dylan. You get to be a superhero and it's great. Our dad got Briley and me into collecting and I wouldn't change it for anything. I mean, I could be spending my money on drugs or mundane stuff. Instead, I buy things that will bring me joy and enhance my collection." Kat paused. She didn't want to sound like a rich asshole, but this was the one thing, besides her family, that brought her great joy.

"I don't understand, but Emma would. She likes dollhouses and has so much furniture for them we've set up shelves in her room to hold all of it. I found a lot of her pieces at yard sales."

"Yard and estate sales are awesome for finding treasures. I've gotten a ton of comics that way. What else does she enjoy? If I'm not crossing a line by asking?"

"You're not. Let's see. She likes those D.C.

superhero dolls and the Lego figurines. She also loves building Lego sets. Her favorites are the Elves Lego sets."

"I love those."

"And I don't mind buying them for her because I know she will take care of them. She wanted the Dragon Sanctuary, but it's retired and out of my price range."

Kat had that set along with almost every other Elves set. Those sets along with the Creator series were her favorite to collect. She didn't think mentioning that would be a good idea, but maybe she could convince Dylan to give it to Emma for Christmas.

"She's also taking to drawing," Dylan continued. "And she loves the Garriety Science Center."

"Briley and Leah love the Science Center. They would get along great." Kat paused to get her bearings. "So, what do you enjoy besides knitting?" Kat settled on the floor and lay back while Stripes climbed on her chest and settled down.

"I enjoy fishing and camping. I don't get to do those things as much as I would like, but, I think, it makes them more special when I do get to do them. My dad takes Emma out a few times a year to bond with her."

"That's great. We camped when we were kids too. I haven't done as much since I became an adult, but I wouldn't be opposed to it. Since Briley and Leah got together, they've been camping and fishing a few times."

"Those are the type of memories I want Emma to have. She has enough going on in her life that I want to try and make everything else as normal as possible."

"Does she have issues fitting in?" It was something she had wondered but didn't want to offend Dylan.

"Not really. She has wonderful friends, but she still has nightmares occasionally and her anxiety flares up from time to time. It's hard to see her sad and scared, but I know she's happy and I try, along with Mom and her therapist, to make sure she is on the right track and I know she is. I don't want her to resent the hand she's been dealt."

"Dylan, you can't beat yourself up; all you can do is try your best and from what I've seen, that's exactly what you're doing."

"Okay, let's get back to easy topics. What's your favorite food?"

Kat answered the question and closed her eyes as Dylan recited what foods she didn't like. Dylan's voice was soothing, and Kat could listen to it all night, but she also knew if she lay on the floor any longer her back would start to protest; however, at the moment she couldn't bring herself to care. Soon, she nodded off to sleep to the lulling sound of Dylan's voice.

Chapter Fourteen

Kat paced in front of Brew and Bake waiting for Dylan to arrive. Last night, she'd fallen asleep on the floor talking with Dylan and woken up stiff. After a five-mile run with Briley and yoga with Griffin, she almost felt like herself again. A cuddle with Stripes after her shower was a much-needed distraction from her lunch with Dylan at eleven.

Before leaving work for lunch, she'd taken the time to put on a shirt over her tank top. Dylan deserved the best, and Kat couldn't wait until she was able to take her out to dinner. Just the two of them.

It was a beautiful day, even though the air had cooled considerably from the previous week. Kat loved it, but she couldn't wait for snow this year. If she was lucky, Dylan and Emma would accept her invitation to accompany her to the Christmas Tree Lighting. It was something she'd started doing with Briley and would love to have Dylan and Emma join them.

A quick glance at her watch let her know two minutes had passed since the last time she'd checked. She nodded at the people passing her by and pushed off the building when she spied Dylan walking down the sidewalk. Dressed in a pair of chinos and a pink sweater, with her hair down, Dylan looked like a vision. Kat was so happy Dylan decided to start spending time with her.

Kat held with care the flower she'd chosen for

today, hoping it was okay. The florist didn't have what she wanted, but she'd settled on a hybrid tea rose. It was a bit corny, but she hoped Dylan knew she meant well.

After getting her bearings, she stepped forward and offered the rose to Dylan, who took it but arched her brow in question.

Kat stuffed her hands in her pockets. "I hope it's okay. It's a hybrid tea rose."

"I know." Dylan smiled, then lifted the rose to her nose and sniffed. "It's gorgeous, Kat. Thank you."

"It means…"

"Heaven sent," Dylan supplied.

"Yes." She opened the door for Dylan and found a seat near the front windows. "So. I'm going to get the ham and cheese and an iced tea. What are you getting?" She looked up to catch Dylan's eyes on her. "You okay?"

"I am." Dylan picked up the menu again and pursed her lips as she scanned the selections. "I'm getting the grilled cheese and a water."

"Good choice." Kat closed her menu then accepted Dylan's and handed them to the waitress, stating their orders. Kat clasped her hands together on top of the table. "Sorry I fell asleep on you last night. Long and tiring day."

"It was late. No worries." Dylan toyed with the salt shaker. "Though someone was vocal right about the time you fell…ah…silent."

Kat blushed in embarrassment, then furrowed her brow. "Oh, that was Stripes, my ferret. He can be vocal when he's happy."

"How long have you had him?"

"Almost a year." Kat relaxed in her chair. "He's

great company and friendly once you get to know him. He's got his own corner of the living room. I have a cat tree set up in there with tubes laid throughout, so he can easily climb. He has free roam in the house, but usually tends to stay on his cat tree and he sleeps in a hammock."

Dylan arched her brow. "He likes to dress up?"

"Well…" Kat gnawed on her lip. "He does look good in his sweaters. You can't knock it until you've met him all dressed up. Wait. How do you know he likes to dress up?"

Dylan coughed. "Your Instagram."

"Really? Well, then I should say I looked you up but didn't find any social media accounts."

"I don't have any."

Kat nodded. "Okay." She steered the conversation back to Stripes. "He looks better in his sweaters in person anyway."

"We'll see." They grew quiet when the waitress set their food down. "Look, I want to apologize for freaking out on you the other day."

Kat placed her hand atop Dylan's. "There's nothing for you to apologize for. Really. We all have our insecurities. I don't think any less of you. In fact, I'm more in awe of everything you've had to do. Some people would have given up a long time ago."

"I almost did."

She said it quietly. Kat's heart pounded in her chest, her expression open to let Dylan know she wasn't judging her.

Dylan swirled the straw in her drink. "I kept a bottle of Vicodin in my nightstand drawer after Ian died. It was so hard, Kat."

For a second, Kat felt faint at the thought of

Dylan giving up on life. "You made it." She didn't want to think about a world without Dylan in it.

"I did and I'm grateful I did. I would have hated to miss out on Emma's life. She's a marvel. No matter what's she's been through, she keeps pushing on." Dylan picked up her sandwich.

"Like her mom?"

Dylan stopped with the sandwich halfway to her mouth then lowered it. "I guess so."

"I know so. Now, let's enjoy our food while it's hot, then I'll take you for ice cream."

"You don't have to get back?" Dylan picked up her pickle and took a bite.

"Not until one. That is…if you want ice cream?" She crossed her fingers.

"Not really in the mood for ice cream." Kat tried to smile through her disappointment. "But," Dylan went on, "I wouldn't say no to some chocolate."

Kat sagged in her seat, then sat up straight. "I know just the place. Briley swears by it."

"I can't wait."

Thirty-five minutes later, lunch was paid for and they headed to their next destination.

"We'll cross here." Kat placed her hand on the small of Dylan's back and guided her across the street.

"C and C?" Dylan asked in surprise.

"Yep. My treat." She ushered Dylan in, then lead her to the chocolate section. "Kids are in school so it's not too busy." Kat pointed at the display case. "What's your poison?" Kat leaned closer to Dylan. "I like the chocolate peanut clusters. That's what I'm getting."

Dylan eyed the case. "I want the chocolate caramels."

"Great choice." Kat approached the case and

ordered four of each. "And can I get a dozen of the animal shaped chocolates? I want them separate from the other two." After paying, Kat followed Dylan's lead outside, then down the sidewalk back toward Brew and Bake. "Park's the other way."

"Since you paid for lunch and got dessert, I'm buying the coffee."

"I take mine black."

"I kind of had a feeling." Dylan's mouth turned up in a slight smile.

Kat leaned back against the building to wait. Everything seemed to be going well and Dylan looked comfortable. It was exactly what she needed to help the rest of her day run smoother. Kat pushed off the wall when Dylan came out. The walk to the small park was a short one from the bakery. They found an empty picnic table and took a seat. Kat passed over Dylan's chocolates and accepted her coffee, then put the other bag beside Dylan.

At Dylan's questioning gaze, Kat hurried on. "For Emma."

Dylan started, touched by the gesture. "That's sweet of you."

"It's the least I can do." Leah had told her she needed to make sure to include Emma in some of their outings even though she wasn't with them. "I hope I didn't overstep?"

"No, it's thoughtful." Dylan popped a chocolate in her mouth and chewed. After she took a sip of coffee, she turned to Kat. "This is the best chocolate I've ever tasted."

"I know, right? Leah swears by the spicy chocolates."

"You all seem close."

Kat rested her arms on the top of the picnic table. "We are. Briley and I have always been close. I wasn't sure about Leah at first. Not because she wasn't great, I just wasn't sure about her and Briley. I was hesitant about the age difference, but our parents had a twenty-year age difference and they worked out. It soon became apparent that they were made for each other. I want that someday."

"Happy ever after?"

"Yes, but not the way you're thinking. I'm not looking for a fairy-tale. I'm looking for someone to spend my life with and everything that entails. The good and the bad. I'm aware relationships take work, but I'm willing to put that in. You know?"

"I do know. Ian and I clicked from the beginning and we worked. It wasn't easy, but I knew it wasn't supposed to be. We were happy."

"He seemed great."

"He was. He had his issues, but we were a team."

"That's what I want. To be a team with someone, but I also know what Bri and Leah put into their relationship. Right now, I'm not sure I have the time for that."

"You're making time for me." Dylan smiled at her and Kat's stomach fluttered.

"Well..." Kat ran her fingers through her hair. "You're worth it. I like what we're doing, Dylan. I hope you do too."

"I do. It's nice having someone else I can talk to besides family and Haley."

"Haley?"

"My co-worker. The woman working next to me at the gala. We get on well and hang out once or twice a month outside of work."

"I'm like that with Kyle. He's great and I'm so glad I hired him." Kat gathered her trash and rubbed her hands together. "So, for next week I was hoping, maybe, we could do something different."

"Like what?" Dylan added her trash to the pile.

"Next week is the week of the food truck extravaganza at the park, as Briley likes to call it. I thought we could take a few hours and explore that." Kat picked up her cup and took a sip to calm her nerves. The longer the silence went on, the more her unease grew. "Or not."

Dylan cocked her head and smiled. "I would like that."

"Really?"

"Really. One thing you should know is that I never say something I don't mean."

"Noted." Kat couldn't stop her smile even if she tried. "So, Thursday at eleven?"

Dylan stood, and Kat followed. "Thursday at eleven."

Chapter Fifteen

"Dylan, sit down," Iris said.

It's not what she wanted to do, but she did as her mom asked and sat beside her on the couch. Today was her third lunch friend date with Kat and she was far more nervous for today than the previous two. For one, they would be spending more time together than any other time, and two, these lunches had felt like dates, real dates, not friend dates.

"Stop overthinking things." Iris squeezed her hand. "Have fun."

"Mom, it's not that simple."

"Of course it is. You're getting to know each other; it's okay to like her. You're friends."

"I wouldn't—"

"You are. You text and talk with her all the time. It's good to see you putting yourself out there. Go and have a good time."

That was easy for her mom to say. The previous night, Emma had asked when she would get to meet Kat and Dylan hadn't known what to say because it was too soon, but on the other hand, they'd already met once before. The last thing she wanted was for Emma to get attached, and maybe hurt if the friendship didn't work out. But she'd promised her she would ask Kat to go to the Garriety Zoo with them on Saturday.

"Besides, today you'll get another flower to add to your collection."

It was sweet that Kat took the time to research flower meanings and Dylan looked forward to what she chose. From the onset, she knew Kat was different than most other people she'd met. She wanted to preserve every moment with her, from journaling, to drying and pressing the flowers. She'd started with the dandelion.

"She's a romantic," Iris said. "I like that."

"I do too." Dylan sighed and picked at the cushion on the couch. "I don't want to rush into anything. Mom, I've been alone a long time. Kat's not like anyone I've ever met before. She's warm, funny, and she listens. Really listens."

Iris patted her cheek. "It's time you started seeing yourself like the rest of us see you. Now, you need to get going. You don't want to be late and you look lovely today. That dress is beautiful."

"Thanks, Mom." Dylan checked her phone and stood. As it was, she was cutting it short getting to the park before their meeting time. "I love you, and I'll see you later." Dylan kissed her on the cheek and bounded out the front door.

It was cooler today, but she'd wanted to look good and had chosen a floral Maxi dress that she'd bought at the Garriety Thrift and Buy the previous weekend out with Emma. At first glance she'd fallen in love with the black dress with a bright and colorful floral print. The kimono sleeves, deep V front, and back neckline had sold her. She wasn't sure about the stretch, striped waistband, but Emma had given her approval. It didn't hurt that she looked good in it too. The ten-dollar price tag was also incentive to bring it home.

Finding a parking spot in the park was more of a challenge then she anticipated, but after fifteen minutes of searching, she found one. While making her way through the crowd, she didn't see Kat. After scanning the area, she sent Kat a text asking her location. Not a few seconds later, she received one back from Kat, informing she would come for her.

Dylan spied Kat before Kat saw her. Dressed in a pair of dark washed skinny jeans, a Garriety Meerkats baseball tee, and well-worn sneakers, Kat looked like the all-American dream. More than a few eyes turned to stare at her. Today she wore her hair as a faux hawk again. Dylan would love to run a hand through it.

She waved when Kat stopped and looked around. Her heart pounded when Kat spotted her, and a smile blossomed.

She noticed Kat didn't have a flower with her.

"I know what you're thinking. No flower," was the first thing Kat said when she approached.

"So, you can read my mind?" She said it with a smile to take the bite out of her words. She was disappointed but didn't want to be too easy to read.

Kat held up her hands. "It's my superpower and I know you're wondering where your flower is. No worries. I planned to pick one up before we part ways. I didn't want it to get smashed."

"So, you're anticipating a long lunch haul."

"Are you kidding? This is awesome." Kat rubbed her hands together and Dylan couldn't help but slip her arm through Kat's. It was the first time she'd initiated this kind of touching, but the moment called for it. She was thankful that Kat didn't miss a beat and guided her toward the first food truck. "How about you pick two and I'll pick two and we'll share."

How much were they going to eat? "Sounds good to me."

An hour later, they were seated at a large picnic

table, but thankfully they had the end to themselves. Dylan wasn't crazy about sharing her table with anyone, but there wasn't anywhere else to sit.

The wide array of food on the table was eclectic. She'd chosen tacos and pot-stickers. Kat had chosen fried chicken pieces with three dipping sauces and a set of four burger sliders. They'd both settled on water to drink. They'd added a basket of French fries because why not. "I'm not sure where to start."

"This is where we start," Kat said, pushing the basket of fried chicken pieces and dipping sauces to the center of the table. She dipped a piece in then held it up. Dylan hesitated for a moment before leaning forward and taking it off Kat's fingers. Kat's wide-eyed look was well worth it.

Dylan held back a chuckle while she chewed. "That was good."

Kat coughed, then hurriedly dipped a chicken piece and popped it in her mouth.

As soon as the chicken was finished, Dylan grabbed the basket of pot stickers and sauce. "Have you ever ordered from this truck before?"

"Nope."

"Me either. So, our first time." Dylan winked and enjoyed the dusting of pink raising up Kat's cheeks.

"Yes, well."

When they were finished, Kat gathered all their trash and threw it away. "How about a walk, then we can think about dessert?"

"Sounds good." Dylan stood and joined her.

"I didn't say anything earlier, but your dress is pretty."

Dylan looked Kat up and down, a small smile playing on her lips. "You don't look so bad yourself."

Kat waved her hand. "Compared to you, I'm underdressed." She frowned at her shirt.

"Don't beat yourself up. You look fine."

Kat led them toward the hill overlooking the river and leaned back against a tree. Dylan leaned back beside her. "I didn't ask before, but how are your flowers doing?" She hoped the flowers had at least taken root. It would be a shame if they hadn't. They were beautiful flowers.

Kat dug out her phone and pulled up photos. "Evan treats them like his babies. He's over at the house before he goes to school to check on them."

Dylan accepted the phone and scrolled through the pictures. When she swiped to the next photo, she stopped. Kat and Briley stood next to each other, but that wasn't what held her attention. No, they were both in workout gear. Their running shorts were red, but where Briley wore a tank top, Kat had on a sports bra. It must have been after a work out because they both glistened with sweat.

"Is something wrong with them?" Kat questioned, then peeked at the phone. "We run."

She knew that. Kat's abs were well-defined and the v that ran into her shorts was the hottest thing she'd ever seen. She handed over the phone when Kat started fidgeting. "Maybe I should start running?" It was something she'd done when younger but had let it go after Ian's car accident. Seeing a ripped Kat gave her a bit of incentive.

"Only if it's something you really want. If it's not, you'll get discouraged. If you want to get more exercise, do something that's fun for you. Trust me. I thought I would enjoy cross fit, but it wasn't for me. Leah refuses to run with us. She takes a spinning class and yoga."

"I have thought about spinning class, but I'm not sure. The last time I joined a gym I was fifty pounds heavier and felt self-conscious."

"That's awesome."

"What?" Dylan looked at her sharply.

Kat held her hands up. "Not the self-conscious part, but that you've lost fifty pounds. It's hard work. You should be proud of yourself. And frankly, people that frequent gyms can be assholes. Leah goes to a spinning studio in downtown Garriety. She refused to join Fitness Elite, because everyone looked and acted like they were better than her. I thought I was going to have to hold Briley back from going down there and telling them all off."

Dylan sighed, then voiced the one question she wondered about. "It doesn't bother you?"

"What?" Kat turned so that she was facing Dylan. Kat reached out and pushed the hair out of Dylan's face, then realized what she was doing and stuffed her hand in her pocket.

"That I'm overweight. You look amazing and it's plain that you work hard on your body. Let's face it, I am, by doctors' standards, overweight. A person who is five-foot-four's ideal weight should be between one hundred and ten and one hundred and thirty-four pounds. I haven't been that small in years. Though, when you think about it, a size ten doesn't seem fat." Dylan laughed, but sobered when Kat ground her teeth together and looked to be composing herself.

Kat turned with her back to the tree to look out over the water. "Have you felt this way since the first time we talked?"

"I always feel this way."

"Okay, look." Kat held her hand out. "Come on." She wiggled her fingers.

Without hesitation, Dylan slipped her hand in Kat's. She tried to tame her pounding heart as Kat led them to a secluded spot. Letting go of Dylan's hand, Kat grabbed her shirt and pulled it over her head to expose her tank top. This move caught Dylan by surprise. Kat laid the shirt on the ground and extended her hand out to Dylan. "May I help you down?"

Kat had taken her shirt off, so she could sit on it. "You didn't have to do that."

"Don't be silly, I didn't want you to ruin your dress."

"It was only ten dollars at a thrift store." Dylan took the offered hand and Kat assisted her to sit.

"Doesn't matter, it looks really nice on you." Kat set cross-legged across from Dylan and reached her hands out for Dylan to take. "First things first. Your weight doesn't bother me, but it seems to bother you. I like you the way you are." She lightly squeezed Dylan's hands. "You're a beautiful woman. Inside and out. I'm not now, nor will I ever be ashamed or embarrassed to be with you. Please, believe me."

"I do." She did. Kat had a way with words, but she always seemed so perfect. Did the woman have any flaws? "I was a size six before Ian had his accident." Kat squeezed her hands in encouragement. "I spent months in the hospital with Emma and there wasn't much to do." She laughed. "My time was taken up with either eating or knitting. Some beautiful scarves and hats came out of that. I made baby size ones and donated them to the nursery in the hospital. I gained so much weight I wasn't even sure who I was anymore. I didn't feel like me. You know?"

"I do. Maybe not weight wise, but I felt dead inside going to work every day when I was a full-time accountant. I felt hollow and like I was going through the motions. Life was stagnant."

"It always felt like I was pushing when the door said pull. Then when someone would come visit Emma, they would bring treats. I ate my thoughts, my feelings, and my fears. When half your world was already dead, and the other half was hanging on by a thread, life doesn't really feel all that important. I told you I thought about ending it." She shook her head. "Suicide. My therapist said I should call it what it was. At the time, it felt right, but there was always something holding me back. Most of the week I would spend sleeping at the hospital, but those other days I would spend in my bed at home. Alone. The temptations were so strong, but then I would pick up the picture of Emma from off the nightstand, shut the drawer with the pain pills, roll over, and go to sleep."

"I can't even imagine what you went through, but it sounds like you got the help you needed. Some people can't and don't want to take that step. That you did and overcame all of that. You're amazing, Dylan, and I wish you could see what I see."

"I wish I did as well." She pulled one hand back and wiped her eyes. "I don't hate myself or my circumstances anymore. It took a couple of years of therapy, but it helped, and I love myself now. Weight and all, but sometimes people are just nice to me to be nice."

"I can't stand those types of people. Smile to your face then stab you in the back when you're turned. For the most part, most of the people I've met here have been great, but a few, well," she shrugged, "I steer clear of them. I started new here and I try to stay positive. I force myself to stay positive. I have to. I'm not at Briley's level of enthusiasm, but I'm working my way up."

"I didn't want this day to delve into deep territory."

"Why not? We're learning about each other. Let's see." Kat tapped a finger on her lips.

She looked cute while she was thinking. Dylan allowed her fingers to play with the palm of Kat's free hand.

"Okay," Kat said, then took a deep breath, letting it out in a sigh. "I've never told anyone this. Not even Briley."

"You don't have to tell me."

"I don't mind. I trust you, Dylan. It's something I feel, and I've chosen not to fight it. I used to drink heavily when I was in college. Briley may have suspected but she never said anything. I got so drunk one night I blacked out. When I woke up, I was in a strange bedroom, with a half-naked woman I'd never seen before. I dressed and stumbled home, disgusted with myself and scared. I didn't want to be that person that didn't know who she was, where she was, or who she was with. I stopped cold turkey and only drink occasionally now. I normally don't go over two. Usually I stick with beer or wine, nothing harder. It was the turning point in my life. Anything could have happened to me. I was lucky it didn't. I'm ninety percent sure I didn't have sex that night, but the fact that it *could* have happened left me with nightmares for months. I finally, at the advice of one of my professors, went to see a therapist. She was a godsend. It was in the top three of the best decisions I've ever made."

Dylan hadn't expected her to be so open. "Thank you for telling me that."

"Anything else you want to know?"

"Therapy was one but what where the other two best decisions?"

"Moving here and eating dinner at the Burger Café." Kat grinned and arched her brow.

"Wow." Dylan took her hands back and dramatically fanned her face. "You're smooth, Kat. So smooth."

Kat snorted. "Only with you, I'm sure." She stood and helped Dylan up, then picked her shirt up and tossed it over her shoulder. "Dessert?"

Dylan caught her top lip between her teeth while she came to a quick decision, then grinned. She slipped her arm through Kat's, who seemed to stand up a bit straighter at their proximity. "Cheesecake?" She was a sucker for cheesecake and for once, she wasn't worried about Kat disliking her weight. If she was sure of one thing, it was how sincere Kat always seemed to be.

Kat grinned. "Yes. I love cheesecake. The second to last food truck sells it." She hesitated. "Ah…about next Thursday…"

"Yes?" She hoped Kat didn't have to work next week. Dylan really was starting to love their Thursday lunches.

"Nothing bad. Briley may be the baker in the family, but I'm the grill master. Would it be too soon to invite you to my house for lunch? Simple food. Maybe steaks and grilled vegetables. You could meet Stripes."

That really wasn't a bad idea. Dylan did want to see her house. Even though she wasn't ready for more than friendship, she enjoyed their time together, but if this was going to be more, she wasn't the only one Kat needed to impress. "How about we leave our regular Thursday lunch just the two of us and the following

Saturday I could bring Emma for the cookout. Would you be okay with that?" Dylan held her breath.

Kat stopped and smiled. "Really?"

"Yes."

"I would love that. If you're sure?"

"I'm sure. Besides, she wants to meet Stripes as well. She had a good laugh looking through your Instagram photos of him and she's googled ferrets. Be prepared for lots of questions."

"That's…" Kat ran her fingers through her hair. "That's great. And don't forget after our cheesecake, we have to get your flower."

"I can't wait to see what you choose." Next Thursday and Saturday couldn't come fast enough.

Chapter Sixteen

For the tenth time, Kat looked over everything to make sure she hadn't forgotten something. Steaks. Check. Vegetables. Check. Grill set up. Check. Flowers. Check. "Okay, Stripes, I think we're ready for them." Stripes didn't look impressed and ran out of the room. "Well, then. Everyone's a critic."

Today was a big day. She'd worked all day yesterday to make sure there would be plenty of time today to spend with Dylan and Emma. Kyle and Reeva had understood. She did feel a bit guilty but all they were doing today was laying flooring in the two tiny houses currently under construction. Kyle had mentioned if they had time, they were going to hang the kitchen cabinets. She kept reminding herself there wouldn't be a set-back for today. She wanted everything to be perfect.

It was her first time, officially, meeting Emma and she didn't want to mess it up. Besides the flower, she'd also gotten Emma a new blind bag Lego figure. She hoped she hadn't overstepped. The last thing she wanted to do was push too much.

"You look more stressed than I expected."

Kat jumped then gripped the countertop. "Shit, Briley. Do you always have to do that?"

Briley leaned against the counter. "It's my right."

"And I'm not stressed."

"You are, but that's okay." Briley patted her on

the back. "You're doing great, Kat. Besides being an amazing human being, you're—" She stopped and tapped her pursed lips. "I'm sure there's more, but you're great, Kat, and she clearly sees that."

"You do always know the right thing to say, Bri."

"That's also what Leah says." Briley picked up three oranges and started juggling until Kat took them away. Briley gripped Kat's upper arms. "I know it's scary. You're getting to spend an extended time with Emma and they're meeting Stripes."

Kat nodded.

"It's going to be okay. I promise."

"Did you just come over to give me a pep talk, or did you need something?"

"Just the pep talk. That's what I'm here for."

"You're great."

"I know. I know." Briley looked at the counter. "Two flowers."

"One's for Emma."

"I'm glad you're happy." Briley backed away and gave her two thumbs up before leaving.

Kat didn't have time to think when not five minutes after Briley left then she heard a car door shut. "Shit, they're here. This is a good thing. A good thing."

She jumped when the doorbell rang and scooped Stripes up, who'd come running down the hall. "It's time, buddy." She kept a firm hold of Stripes then pulled the door open. Emma was in front and Dylan had her arms wrapped around her shoulders. "I'm so glad you two are here. Come in." She ushered them in and some of her nerves dissipated at Dylan's smile.

"We're glad to be here too. Aren't we, Emma?"

"Yes. We brought dessert. Can I pet him? I've read a lot of articles about ferrets." She pointed at

Stripes.

"That's cool. Let's sit down and I'll introduce you." Kat sat at the end of the couch while Emma sat in the middle and Dylan on the other end. Kat had moved some things around in the living room to make it easier for Emma to maneuver if she used her crutches or wheelchair instead of her prosthetic. "This," Kat held up Stripes, "is Stripes. Stripes, this is Emma and Dylan."

"I read where ferrets like to play with cat toys?" Emma asked and touched the top of Stripes head with the tip of her finger.

"He has so many toys. Briley, my sister, is always buying him new ones. He sleeps in a hammock at night and his favorite toy is a tiny hedgehog cat toy. He carries it everywhere."

Emma laughed. "Why is he named Stripes if he doesn't have any?"

Kat relaxed back against the couch with a contented Stripes staring at their guests. "I let my three-year-old niece, Griffin, name him."

"Can I hold him?"

"Sure. If your mom says okay." Kat looked to Dylan for permission.

"It's fine with me," Dylan said, looking over Emma's shoulder.

"You have to be gentle with him, but once you get to know each other, he'll be all over you."

"I will be."

Kat handed over a quiet Stripes and relaxed when Stripes settled onto Emma's lap. "He likes to have the top of his head and under his chin scratched. Later, if you want, I will show you his playroom."

"I'd like that." Emma ran her fingers along his

fur then under his chin. Stripes flopped on his belly to have Emma scratch it.

"He only does that with people he likes." She looked up and caught Dylan's gaze. Today she wore a pair of jeans and a blue t-shirt. Her hair was up, and she looked comfortable. That's what Kat wanted. She didn't want Emma or Dylan to feel like they weren't wanted. "You look nice. You both do. I mean—"

"You as well. I believe we were thinking along the same lines." Dylan pointed to Kat's t-shirt. "It is a cookout."

"Yes, it is." Kat stood. "I'll be right back." She hurried into the kitchen, grabbed the flowers, and the toy. "You've got this. They're here. They came," she said, quietly. When she turned from the counter, she jumped back. "You scared me." Dylan stood in the doorway.

"You look nervous. Are you nervous?"

"A little." In fact, she felt a nervous flutter in her stomach. "I understand this day for what it is. I know bringing Emma wasn't an easy decision to make."

"Actually, it was an easy decision. I don't understand it myself, but it was the right time." Dylan took a step forward and looked at the items in Kat's hands.

"Oh." She thrust one of the flowers at Dylan. "This is yours. Honestly, I didn't pick this for any special meaning, I thought it was beautiful, and you're obviously beautiful. So…"

Dylan stared at the apricot, yellow, and orange rose, then up to Kat. "Sometimes, the meaning isn't always important, but the intent behind it. Thank you, Kat. It's truly beautiful. And that one?"

"So, I figured I would get Emma one as well.

That's stupid, right?" She grimaced. "Of course it is. She's a kid. Why would she want one?"

"Kat." Dylan touched her arm. "Take a deep breath for me. Let it out. It's a lovely gesture and I'm sure she'll love it. And the Lego?"

"She collects them. So, I thought I would get one to add to her collection." She hadn't been this worked up in a while. What was wrong with her? "I'm not always like this. I swear. My nerves are getting the better of me."

"I know, and I can tell. You should give them to her."

"I will."

Dylan walked ahead of her and sat beside Emma, who held a content Stripes in her lap. Kat sat on the other end of the couch.

"Mom, you got another flower." Emma lit up.

"I did. Isn't it pretty?"

"Yes."

"Um, here." Kat handed Emma her flower and Lego blind bag. "I got you one as well and a Lego blind bag. Your mom told me how much you like them. The rose, well, I love hot chocolate and that's the name of this rose. I thought most kids like hot chocolate." Kat fiddled with the hem of her shirt when Emma looked at the items, then back up to her.

"Thank you. No one's ever given me a flower before."

"You're welcome."

"Mom, can you put my flower with yours?"

"I can." Dylan placed them both on the coffee table, along with Emma's toy.

"You said something about dessert?" Kat asked. This was more nerve-wracking than when she signed the papers for her business.

Emma nodded. "Yes. We made it this morning. It's in my bag."

Dylan picked the bag up and pulled out a sealed container before handing it to Kat. "It's banana pudding."

"I love banana pudding. It'll go perfect with our meal. I've already got everything set up outside. Let me light the grill and I'll get our lunch cooking. You ladies are welcome to join me outside or stay in here. If you come outside, I'm going to be occupied, so Stripes has to stay in here."

"Will he be lonely?" Emma asked with a little frown that melted Kat.

"Nope. Stripes likes his alone time. Besides, he has plenty of toys to play with. Though, there was one time I went outside and looked back at the door and he had his little nose pressed up against the glass. I felt so guilty, I gave him two dinners."

"He conned you?" Dylan's grin and tone conveyed amusement.

"I couldn't help it; he looked so pitiful."

"I'll go out with you," Emma said.

Kat lifted Stripes off her and set him on the back of the couch. "Let's go." She held up the container of banana pudding. "I'm going to put this in the fridge." Kat put the pudding away then handed Dylan the tray of steaks. "I hope steaks are okay?"

"They're fine. We both like steak," Dylan said and Emma nodded.

Kat had debated about what cut to go with but wanted this lunch to go well so she'd settled on filet-mignon. The butcher had such a good price on them, she couldn't pass it up. Kat grabbed the veggies and held the door open for Emma. "Watch your step."

Once outside, they set the food on the table and Kat slipped her apron on, then lit the grill and proceeded to twirl the tongs. "You ladies are in for a treat. I'll fix the veggies first, because they'll take longer than the steaks."

Kat looked toward Emma, who motioned her over. With Kat now standing close, Emma indicated for her to lean down, and when she did, Emma kissed her on the cheek.

"Uh…"

"Your apron, silly," Emma said, then sat back down.

Kat frowned then looked down at her apron that had 'Kiss the Cook' in bright red letters. She was going to kill Briley. "Briley must have switched them out," Kat said.

"What was the other apron?" Dylan asked.

"Harley Quinn."

"Of course." Dylan stood. "While you cook, would you mind if Emma and I checked out the flowers?"

"Not at all. Watch your step, though. Evan has plans for the stone walk around the flowers but hasn't gotten to it yet."

"We will." Dylan squeezed her arm, then helped Emma down the three steps leading off the deck. Kat placed the tinfoil wrapped corn on the cob and potatoes on the grill, then closed the lid. She enjoyed having them there and it wasn't as awkward as she'd expected. She could do this. They could do this. She knew it.

❧❧❧❧

Dylan hummed and made sure Emma stepped carefully while they looked at Kat's flowers. Her backyard was on the smaller side but beautiful and well maintained.

What she hadn't expected was for Kat to be so nervous. It was cute. She also hadn't expected Kat to give Emma a rose. No one had ever done that for Emma before. Kat was so genuine it blew her away.

"Mom."

"What, sweetie?" Dylan pushed the hair out of Emma's eyes.

"Kat's your friend now."

"She is."

Emma nodded. "Can she be mine?"

"I don't see why not. You'll have to ask her, but I'm sure she won't mind." That was a good thing. Hopefully. It was both a blessing and a curse. Now, she would have to make sure that her baby didn't end up hurt if something went sideways.

"Okay, I will. She's nice."

"She is."

"And pretty." Emma looked up at her.

"She is."

"Good."

Emma must have gotten what she wanted because she was quiet as they headed back to the deck after walking the fence line. Dylan loved watching Emma be sure in her steps. She really was a pro with the prosthetic now. She would never let her fall, but always held out until she knew Emma needed the help.

"Let me help you, little lady." Kat walked over to them and waited until Emma gave the okay, then helped her up the last step.

Dylan was surprised but she shouldn't have been. Kat seemed to always know what to say and do. As she stepped onto the deck, on impulse, Dylan kissed

Kat on the cheek. Not waiting for her reply, she joined Emma at the table.

"Okay," was all Kat said with a pleased look before she set two pitchers on the table. "Water and lemonade. If you want something else, let me know."

"This is perfect," Dylan said.

Emma nodded. "I want some lemonade."

Dylan poured them both a glass, then watched Kat at the grill. She looked like she belonged. "How long have you been grilling?"

"Since I was young. I would always help my dad when we'd grill. He taught me everything he knew then I read up. It's fun. Briley can't grill to save her life and I can't bake. So, it all worked out. Especially since we live across the street from each other."

"I didn't know that."

"Yep. Her house used to be directly across from mine until she moved in with Leah, who lives beside Briley's old house. It's on the market and we hope someone nice moves in."

"How did you come about this house?" She decided to keep today calm and informative.

"The man that used to live here had a stroke and he moved in with his son. Briley's friend helped me get it at a good price. I've been working on renovating it since I moved in. I love it."

"It's a beautiful house."

"It's nice," Emma added. "Mom said you like Legos."

"Yes." Kat turned the corn then focused on Emma. "I love putting them together. Your mom tells me you like the Elf ones."

Emma nodded. "Yup. I have the completed ones on a shelf, and I put the Lego figures in my dollhouses."

"That's so cool. Lego Han, hanging out with Lego cop, hanging out with Lego Wonder Woman. Who wouldn't want to live in a house like that?"

Emma giggled. "They love it."

"I would too. How many dollhouses do you have?"

"I have three. Santa got me one. Papa got me the other one and Mom let me get one at a yard sale."

"I got some really cool superhero figures at a yard sale last month. It was great. They were a little worn, but still awesome. I have them on a shelf in my office."

"Can I see them?"

"Sure. After we eat, I'll show them to you."

Emma bounced in her seat. "I like the D.C. hero dolls. I have bunches."

"I have bunches of figures too. I can picture them hanging out with Stripes after I go to sleep at night."

Emma giggled, and Dylan wasn't sure what she was so worried about. Kat was a natural.

"Mine party together," Emma said.

"Mine do too. They party hard. Probably swing from the ceiling fan." Emma and Kat both started laughing.

They continued talking about their figures as Dylan watched. It was nice seeing Emma so carefree. Kat wasn't just talking to her; she was having a silly conversation and it warmed her heart. She wouldn't be the one to end this. Unless something catastrophic happened. Not that she could see that happening. She didn't want anything more right now, just friendship. But seeing how well her daughter and Kat got along, she would have a hard time saying no to something more. For now, she would ride the tide of where they were headed and enjoy the journey. They both deserved that much.

Chapter Seventeen

The next couple of months passed in a blur for Kat as her life settled into a pleasant routine. Monday mornings were reserved for breakfast with Briley. Thursday mornings were her standing date with Griffin and yoga. Still occurring was her one-on-one time with Leah and Evan. She also made it a point to have lunch with Dylan a few times a week.

Work ran smoothly but started to take up most of her time. Time she could have spent with her new favorite girl. The last two Saturdays she had planned to spend with Dylan, but canceled due to two work deadlines. Kat loved seeing the joy in her customers' eyes the first time they saw their tiny house.

Still, it sucked that time with Dylan was sacrificed. She was considering hiring another employee, but now it wasn't feasible. She knew Dylan was still holding back and that was okay. They didn't need to know every detail of their life stories yet.

Texting with Dylan had become a daily occurrence, and their nightly talks were a must, but it still didn't seem like enough. She missed her. Missed spending time with her and Emma. Making new memories. They were supposed to have dinner together the following weekend. It would be the first time she'd had dinner with Dylan and Emma. But, not today, today was for work.

Today, she and Kyle were on their way out of

the city to check out an old dilapidated barn that the owners wanted to sell. They hoped for salvageable wood boards to use for flooring in their tiny homes. What an awesome find that would be. Kat loved the look of repurposed wood and so did her clients. The asking price seemed low. Hopefully that wasn't a tactic to get them down there and then jack up the price.

"From what we saw in the pictures, the wood looked good; hopefully that's the case," Kyle said, drumming his fingers on the dash. "I would love to make some cabinets with that wood."

"They would look fantastic. I hope it's worth our time." They'd driven for an hour, and still had forty-five minutes to go. Hitched to the truck was a trailer for any wood ready to take back with them. If they bought the barn, their plan was to return another day to tear it down and haul the salvageable wood back to the company yard.

Kyle opened his water bottle and took a sip. "It would be cool to find some treasures inside."

The lady on the phone had promised that if they wanted the barn, they could have everything inside. Her husband had died five years ago, and it was too much for her to maintain the upkeep. The space, she said, where the barn stood would make a fantastic garden.

"I can't believe it's almost Fall," Kat said. The time had sped by and Halloween would be here before she knew it. Already, Leah had almost finished her family's costumes, and they were keeping mum.

After eating dinner one night with Dylan, Kat asked if they wanted to be part of her costume idea this year and Dylan had reluctantly agreed for Emma's sake. Kat had promised to keep it simple. After racking her mind, Kat decided to go with an oldie but goodie. Baseball players. Stylish, but still nothing too extravagant for Dylan. Her idea had gone over swimmingly.

"So," Kyle said. "How's it going with your girl?"

After a night out, she confided in Kyle and Reeva about Dylan and Emma. They both seemed happy for her, then she and Kyle had to listen to Reeva's dating woes for the next hour. She'd corrected him many times about them only being friends, but he'd waved her off, telling her he wasn't blind. "Good. We have dinner plans with Briley and company tonight."

"Is it the first time with you all together?"

"It is with Evan and Emma."

"Your family's good people. You don't have anything to worry about. Are you worried?"

Kat sighed, slowed the truck, and took the next exit. "Not worried, but it is the first time in almost two months that we've all spent any time together. It's nerve wracking." She pulled into the nearest gas station and parked. "I need a coffee. You coming in?"

"A coffee sounds good."

Ten minutes later, they were back on the road with their coffees, Kat's chocolate donuts, and Kyle's beef jerky and peanut M&M's.

"Too bad your sister didn't send a basket of treats for us," Kyle remarked.

"I tried to catch her in time, but she'd already divided them up and my house wasn't one of her stops." Briley would bake weekly then make baskets to give her neighbors and the employees at the Garriety nursing home.

"Bummer."

"What about you? Are you still seeing that

woman from the grocery store?"

"No." He popped a few M&M's into his mouth. "She got back with the ex."

"Bummer," Kat repeated.

The rest of the ride was in silence. They both perked up when Kat pulled down a long, dusty, gravel road and the house and the barn came into view. The pictures didn't do it justice. The barn was huge. Part of the roof had caved in and an entire wall covered the ground. The grass was overgrown, and a few vultures were perched atop of what was left of the roof. It was an eerie yet beautiful sight.

Once they were parked, Kat hopped out, pulled out her camera from the backseat, and took several pictures of the barn both in color and black and white. She zoomed in and took several pictures of the vultures. It was in incredible sight and she couldn't even imagine how many memories were made in the barn and surrounding land.

Kat lowered the camera when Kyle patted her on the shoulder and motioned with his head to the house. They made their way across the lawn toward an older woman who waited for them. Kat held out her hand. "I'm Kat and this is Kyle."

"Good to finally put faces to the names. I'm Brenda." She took a step back and sat on one of the rocking chairs on the porch. "You both can head on over. I'm going to wait here."

"Thank you, ma'am," Kyle said.

Kat slipped the camera strap over her neck, allowing the camera to settle by her side. She made her way across the field while Kyle grabbed the weed eater. Fifteen minutes later, he had a small area around the downed barn wall clear. Most of the boards were in fantastic shape.

"We can use these," Kyle said.

"This is awesome," Kat said. "Clear an area around the door, then we'll explore inside." Kyle did that, then they carefully made their way inside. "Crap." There was an old tractor and dozens of large pieces of farm equipment crammed into the center of the barn. Long counters ran along three walls with shelves filled to the brim.

"This is more than I expected." He tugged at his beard. "I mean, I know a guy who could take the tractor and some of this other stuff off our hands. He refurbishes farm equipment like this and donates it to organizations that can't afford them."

"That's really cool. We won't have any use for them. Will he be able to come and get them or would we have to arrange for them to be delivered?"

"He'd come get them."

"The beams also look like they're in good condition."

Kyle knocked on a wood pillar. "Some wood is rotted, but the majority is in good condition. I think this would be a good buy."

Kat took another look around. "As long as the price stays the same. Let's take a walk around the outside, then go and talk with Brenda."

"Sounds good, boss. I'll grab the weed eater."

As soon as they turned a corner of the barn and got a look at the backside, Kat stopped in her tracks. Situated against the side of the barn and covered in tall weeds was a camper. A small, seen better days camper, but still a camper.

"Clear a path to the door of the camper." Once it was clear, Kat grabbed a hold of the door and opened it. The roof was caved in at parts and there was water damage, not to mention the smell, but the bones of the camper looked to be in good condition. "This is perfect. I wonder if she'll include it in the sale of the barn?"

Kyle looked skeptical. "You want this? We build tiny houses."

"It's for Dylan and Emma. They have been thinking about buying one and I mentioned I would help them redo it, but Dylan said she didn't have the money to buy one."

He patted her on the shoulder. "It'd be for your girls. Nice."

She didn't bother to correct him as they made their way back to the house. Brenda was waiting for them with a pitcher of lemonade and three glasses. Kat accepted hers and leaned back against the porch railing. "You said on the phone that everything inside was included with the sale. Does that also include everything outside?"

"The downed wall is included."

Kat took a sip of her drink. "What about the camper?"

Brenda kicked her rocker into motion. "I forgot about that. My Fred bought that years ago. He had a plan to renovate it and we'd explore with it, but he became sick not long after that. What would you want it for? Redo it and sell it?"

"No. I have a friend who wants to find a camper and redo it so she and her daughter can go camping. She doesn't have the money to buy one, but if we can work it into the sell, then I'd give it to her."

"It's not in good shape," Brenda said.

"I know." Kat placed her empty glass back on the

tray. "I told her we could make it a group project. Me, her, and her daughter."

Brenda tilted her head and a smile blossomed across her face. "You can have the camper." She held up her hand to stop Kat from objecting. "Now, let's talk about the sale of the barn." Thirty minutes later, Kat had handed over a check for the barn, then carried the tray into the kitchen per Brenda's request.

"Kat," Brenda said, once they were in the kitchen. "You should bring your family and that camper around when you get it finished. It would do my heart good."

Kat rubbed the back of her neck. "They're not my family. At least not like that."

"I may be an old woman, but I'm not blind, dear."

"No, I guess you're not." Kat held her hand out, but Brenda drew her into a hug. "I'll bring them by."

"Good. Now go, you have a few good hours to load some things into your truck before it starts getting dark."

"All right."

Both worked in unison to load all the loose wood into the trailer and piled boxes and loose tools into the bed of the truck. Not much of a dent was made, but once the bigger pieces were moved, they would finish faster. They'd planned to sell the smaller pieces of farm equipment and the tools they didn't want at the Garriety trade sale in a few weeks' time. Hopefully, they'd make back a bit of the money spent on the barn. If they had time after they'd cleared the barn, they'd both decided to help Brenda get the ground ready for her garden.

She grabbed the rag out of her back pocket and wiped her face. "Did you give your buddy a call?"

Kyle nodded. "He's going to join us here

tomorrow morning. He's also going to help us load the camper. Hopefully, all will go well, and we'll be done in a few days. Since we're giving him all the bigger machine pieces, he's agreed to bring a couple guys to help us tear down the barn. All he requested was drinks and snacks on hand."

"Now that," Kat said with a grin, "I can do." She downed her water. "Let's get out of here. By the time we get home it shouldn't be too late, and we can get this stuff unloaded. I should have the time for a shower before dinner."

"Sounds good to me."

She leaned back in her seat as Kyle drove. She wasn't as anal as Briley about who drove her truck. The barn was a good buy, and she hoped Dylan could see as much potential in the camper as she did. The barn would take up all her time this week, so tonight would be the only time she had to spend with Dylan and Emma until Saturday. That's when she would show them the camper and get their ideas about how to refinish it. She didn't want to think too much on the family project idea, but it sure felt good to think of them like that. Slow and steady, Kat. Slow and steady.

Chapter Eighteen

Dylan stood in her bedroom in front of the mirror and lifted her hair, debating whether to wear it up or down. Dinner with Kat's family the previous Friday had turned out good. She liked Leah, and Briley was always good fun. Evan acted respectful, and Griffin was a ball of sunshine. Today Kat had promised them a surprise. Kat seemed excited enough for all three of them. Even Briley couldn't get the surprise out of her and she'd tried, countless times.

Emma kept badgering her to spend more time with Kat, but first Dylan had to be sure Kat was going to stick around and so far, she hadn't shown any signs of running. Dylan felt it was the right time for Kat and Emma to spend more time together.

"Mom, can you help with my pants?" Emma called out from her bedroom.

"Coming." From all the times Kat and Emma had talked over the phone, they got along thick as thieves. Dylan knew if she and Kat continued down the path they were on, that it would lead to more, but Emma's well-being was always in the back of her mind. It would devastate Emma if Kat suddenly left their lives. If Dylan was being honest, it would devastate her too.

Their nightly talks were one of the things Dylan looked forward to the most. Kat was a creature of habit and every night at nine thirty, Dylan's phone would ring. Every time they hung up, it left her wanting more, but she was afraid to take the next step. She had to be sure, and right now she wasn't a hundred percent sure.

Dylan winked at her image in the mirror, then walked into Emma's room and helped her put her pink shorts on over her prosthetic.

"What do you think the surprise is?" Emma asked.

"I don't know. Let's grab our picnic stuff, then meet Kat at her business." Emma was vibrating as much now as Kat was last night. Whatever it was, she hoped Emma wasn't disappointed.

Dylan gratefully accepted the picnic basket her mom handed her.

"Go. Have fun," Iris said.

"Bye, Grams."

"Bye, Mom."

"Bye, my darlings."

The ride to Kat's business was quick and easy, even though she'd never been there before. For the few lunch dates they'd been on, Kat always insisted on joining her at Brew and Bake. After their first few meetings, Dylan had explained to Kat her financial situation because she didn't want Kat to pay for everything, but she wouldn't be able to eat out every time they got together for lunch. Kat was more than accommodating, insisting that she could make lunch and bring it to her. In the end, both agreed that if they continued seeing each other at lunch, they would alternate who paid or brought the food. It had worked out well. The light teasing she'd received from her co-workers when Kat would come by during the week was a fair price to pay to spend thirty minutes in Kat's company.

The one thing that had stood out was that Kat didn't show her one ounce of pity; instead, her eyes had conveyed a level of compassion she rarely saw. It was another note to add to the list of Kat being too good to be true.

In front of one of the buildings, Kat talked to a man around their age. It looked to be Kyle from the picture Kat had showed her. Kat had mentioned she wanted Dylan and Emma to feel safe at her business and showed her pictures of Kyla and Reeva, so they knew who to look for if Kat wasn't around.

She parked in front of the building. By the time she and Emma had exited the car, Kat was waiting for them.

"Emma." Kat drew Emma into a tight hug, then did the same with Dylan. "You both are right on time." Quickly, she looked them over. "And look fantastic."

Emma grabbed Kat's arm. "Don't keep us waiting."

"Follow me then." Kat held the door open for them and allowed them both to walk through. One of the things Dylan had learned about spending time with Kat was that she was well-mannered.

Dylan slipped her arm through Kat's. They'd been touching more recently, and Dylan couldn't say she was upset about that. It was nice.

"Okay." Kat patted Dylan's arm, then untangled herself, positioned Dylan and Emma in front of her and took a couple of steps back. "Okay." She ran a hand over the top of her hair, Dylan noticing it looked like it had recently been trimmed.

"Kat?" Dylan pulled Emma back against her chest.

"Okay. As you know, we recently tore down a barn." They both nodded. "Well, there was something else there as well. Dylan, I hope I haven't overstepped but I thought we could work on it together. It would be yours, of course, I have the title, you can have it, but I had hoped we could redo it together."

With each word out of Kat's mouth, Dylan's heart rate picked up. There was only one thing they'd talked about working on together. "Kat."

"Before you say anything you should know that it was free. It needs a ton of work. It has potential. Please. I wanted to do something nice for you. You both have brought so much joy into my life."

Dylan closed her eyes and hugged Emma tighter.

"What is it, Mom?" Emma asked.

Kat knew she didn't have the money to pay for a camper. Kat's sad eyes and pout had its desired effect on Dylan. "It was free?"

"Yes."

"And it needs work?"

"I promise." Kat held her arms out to her sides. "Tons."

"And you're going to help with said work?" There was no way she would be able to do it by herself. She didn't know the first thing to do and would have to rely on Kat.

"Absolutely." Kat grinned.

Dylan held Emma out at arm's length. "Remember last year when we talked about maybe getting a camper and traveling around?"

"Yes." Emma looked from her mom to Kat. "You got us a camper?"

"Well, this lady gave it to me. I'm hoping we can work on it together."

"Like a family?" Emma brightened.

"I…" Kat bit her lip.

"Friends can be family," Dylan threw out, letting Kat off the hook even though the blush rushing up her cheeks was a nice look.

"Yes, friends can be family," Kat said, then

rubbed her hands together. "Ready?"

"Lead the way. This is your show, after all," Dylan said.

"Come on."

Dylan followed behind them, coming to a complete stop when they walked behind the tiny house that was being worked on. Then her sight focused in the corner of the building where the ugliest camper she had ever seen sat. The camper looked big enough for them both, but Kat wasn't exaggerating when she said it needed work. Part of the roof was caved in, and the two windows she could see were smashed out. Clunks of grass liberally coated the outside of the camper. This contraption looked like it needed to be in the dump and not remodeled. Watching Kat keep pace with Emma with huge smiles on their faces melted any doubts she had about the camper. With a sigh, Dylan came to terms with her fate.

Both Kat and Emma excitedly bounded around the camper. Dylan chuckled at their exuberance. Kat wasn't like anyone she'd ever met before and it was so refreshing.

"I know what you're thinking," Kat said, holding her hands up and drawing Dylan out of her thoughts.

"I'm not sure you do." Dylan smiled at her, then nodded toward the camper, before slipping her hand in Kat's. The blinding smile on Kat's face told her all she needed to know. "Let's join my daughter and see what we're up against."

"It's great, Dylan. Truly. You'll be blown away."

Two hours later, Dylan hadn't been blown away, but they all had ideas about what should be done to the camper. Kat had promised there would be room for two beds, a small kitchenette, and a tiny bathroom.

Where Kat said tiny, Dylan knew it would be more like miniscule. Up close, the camper was bigger than she had expected. It would more than do for what she had in mind. Even with all the work needed.

She drove behind Kat's truck and looked to the passenger seat where her daughter would normally be. Emma had asked to ride with Kat and Dylan had agreed because she knew Kat was a responsible driver. If she and Kat were going to become more than friends, Kat needed to spend time with Emma.

After parking, they made their way to an empty spot beside a large oak tree in the park and set up the blanket and picnic basket.

"I can't wait to get started," Emma said when they were all settled.

"Saturday will come before we know it," Kat said, after leaning back against the tree and stretching her legs out in front of her.

"I know." Emma groaned. "When do you think we'll be finished?" Emma accepted the plate of food from Dylan filled with a sandwich, chips, a dill pickle, and a little bit of potato salad and settled it on her lap.

Kat accepted her plate from Dylan with a grateful smile, then answered Emma. "It's hard to say, but we'll get her where she needs to be."

Dylan made her plate, content to eat and listen to them both talk. Even the dogs barking and children playing in the distance couldn't dampen her good mood. After the food was finished, and everything was cleaned up, Emma declared a nap was in order and lay at the foot of the blanket, quickly falling asleep.

"She tires easily," Dylan said. "When we do work on the camper, please keep that in mind."

"Hey," Kat said, and Dylan turned to her. "You

don't have to worry about that. I've noticed how tired she gets during the times I've spent with her. You'll be there and if she gets tired, I have a pull-out couch in my office she can take a nap on. I would never let anything happen to her if it's within my power."

Dylan frowned and shook her head. "You always seem to know the right thing to say."

"I say the wrong things all the time. You're just not around to hear them. Trust me. Briley lets me know. I think she may be keeping a list."

Dylan grew quiet. She didn't want to say something snippy. Kat really was amazing, and it was her own insecurities that were getting the best of her. They sat in silence. Dylan kept still when she felt Kat's arm circle her shoulders. Kat scooted over until their sides were touching.

"Is this okay?"

"It's fine." Dylan reached up and took Kat's hand that was resting on her shoulder, then tangled their fingers together. "I like you, Kat, and I know we're on the road to more…but I don't want to rush anything. I like being friends, and if things slowly go into something more, I would be okay with that. For now, I want things to keep going like they are. Us continuing to get to know each other."

"Natural progression," Kat said.

"Yes. I can't promise you dates or even a set amount of time. I like what we've been doing, and I'd like to continue that way. I can't promise you a future."

Kat slipped her other arm around Dylan's waist and rested their heads together. "Can you promise me another tomorrow?"

With eyes closed, Dylan grasped Kat's arm around her waist. "Yes."

"And a tomorrow after that?"

"Yes."

"That's all I need for now. You're the only woman I want to spend time with."

"Ditto."

"Good."

Dylan sighed when Kat kissed her head. She pulled back slightly to look at Kat's face. "So, what exactly are we doing?"

"Friends with the option for more."

"I like that. Does this mean we're exclusive?" Dylan motioned with her hand from herself to Kat.

"I would like to be, but I understand if you want to keep your options open," Kat said.

"Kat, you're my only option."

Kat arched her brow. "Gee, you make it sound so special."

She knew Kat was joking but could hear the underlining hurt in her voice. Dylan turned enough to see Kat's eyes, and her breath hitched at the intensity she saw in them. Without censoring herself, she reached up and cupped Kat's cheek, caressing her jaw with her thumb. "You're the best option."

Kat held Dylan's hand in place. "I wasn't looking for a relationship, but I'm glad I met you. You're my best option too."

Dylan started to pull her hand back, but Kat caught it and kissed the palm. "Jesus, when did we turn into saps?" Dylan asked. The feelings swirling in the pit of her stomach felt like nothing she'd ever experienced before.

"Somewhere between the sandwiches and the potato salad," Kat deadpanned.

Dylan tried to hold her laugh in but failed, then

leaned forward and drew Kat into a hug.

"Since we're on this subject, there was something I was thinking about," Kat said. Dylan leaned back so she could look in Kat's eyes. "You don't know this about me, but I'm an avid Pinterest searcher."

Dylan feigned shock. "What?"

"I know. I know." Kat sighed. "It's a burden I'm willing to bear."

"Smartass." Dylan tapped the tip of Kat's nose.

"Anyway, I came across something I think would be good for us. If you want."

"Us. As in you and me, or me, you, and Emma?"

"Actually." Kat tightened her hold around Dylan. "It would be me and you." She leaned forward and kissed Dylan lightly on the cheek, then pulled back and glanced at Emma. "And me and Emma. I think if this is going to work, then I need to spend one-on-one time with each of you. I understand you're trying to protect Emma and I get it."

"I…" Dylan closed her mouth when Kat shook her head.

"For the first few months, Emma and I can spend time in your presence. We can play Legos, but I want to expand on that. Emma and I wouldn't venture outside of your house until you okayed it. I never want to push those boundaries."

Dylan relaxed in Kat's arms, who looked way too serious. At this point, Dylan trusted Kat enough to know that she wouldn't steer them the wrong way and it was time that she and Emma spent more time together. "What is it you want to do?"

"Here's my plan. Over the course of the next year, I will create individual envelopes for each of you. On the first day of each month you both will open your envelope and we'll find the time during the month to complete said project. A few things will have to be scheduled, but I'll make sure they're done on a weekend."

Year? Instead of being freaked out that Kat planned to be around for the next year, Dylan was excited. To know Kat was in this long term meant so much, and it was clear the other woman didn't have any issue promising her and Emma the next year. "Like?"

"Like. For Emma. A day of horseback riding. The Science Center. Shopping for camper supplies. Pizza and movie night. Baking and decorating cookies, Legos, maybe creating some new things for her dollhouses."

"Okay." Dylan giggled at Kat's enthusiasm. How did she get so lucky to find a woman like Kat? "What about me?"

"Dinner and a movie, dancing, indoor picnic, museum." Kat bit her lip and whispered in Dylan's ear. "I can't give all my secrets away. I'll run everything for Emma by you, but our dates, well, I want some of those to be surprises. We may not be able to spend as much time together as we like, but I think we can manage a date a month."

"I think we can do better than that." Dylan lifted her hand and ran her fingers down Kat's jawline. "I like surprises. I'll warn you though, just knowing you as long as I have, you have your work cut out for you. You've already set the bar high."

"I have, have I?" The smile that lit up Kat's face set Dylan's heart racing. "I'm willing," Kat said.

"So am I."

With a shared smile, they pulled apart and settled back against the tree, Kat's arm still wrapped around Dylan's shoulders. Dylan wasn't sure how it was going to work, but she knew she wanted it to.

Chapter Nineteen

Over the next few days, Kat had run all her ideas for the envelopes by Dylan, who had okayed all but one of them for Emma. Kat had no issue changing it to something else. Scrapbooking wasn't Kat's thing, because the end product would never look like the picture she'd seen, but Briley had volunteered herself for the job. Briley had promised to come by at seven for dinner and a crash course in crafting. Sometimes, Briley went overboard, and Kat was surprised Leah hadn't yet gone insane with everything Briley sprung on her.

  Kat loved her sister but knew Briley would bring over way too much and would insist everything be picture perfect. On some things, Kat would agree, but the envelopes were going to be ripped open anyway. But she wasn't about to rain on Briley's parade. Especially considering Briley had taken the last few cancellations of their sister night so well. Dylan, on the other hand, had insisted Kat spend some time with her sister, letting her know she didn't want to monopolize all of Kat's free time, even though Kat wanted her to.

  Kat relaxed back into the couch cushion with Stripes on her lap. A smile emerged when she recalled Emma meeting him for the first time. They both took to each other, much to Kat and Dylan's relief. Stripes sometimes had a rough time with new people, but not Emma. He still hadn't warmed up to Dylan yet, but things were progressing nicely, and Kat made sure that her thoughts never strayed to the pessimistic side of things. She'd taken that route with plenty of other relationships and refused to with Dylan. No, Dylan wasn't like anyone she'd ever met before and it was refreshing.

"Boo!"

Kat jumped, almost sending a hissing Stripes flying. She glared at Briley, who smirked at her. "Asshole."

Briley whistled while setting two boxes on the coffee table. "I bet I can guess who you were thinking about." She flopped on the couch beside Kat and picked Stripes up, setting him on her lap and stroking his coarse hair.

"Well." Kat bumped Briley's shoulder. "Now you know what I had to look at when you were starting out with Leah." There was no reason to deny what Briley could see clearly. She was happy and didn't care who knew.

"I like seeing you happy."

"It's…" Kat sighed. "It's not like anything I've felt before. I've always felt content in my past relationships but kept a bit of myself back. With Dylan, I don't want to do that. I want to tell her everything and learn everything about her. It's exciting. So exciting."

Briley grinned and propped her legs up on the coffee table. "I understand. Leah isn't like anyone I've ever met before. I wanted to dive head first and did. It was the best decision I've ever made."

Kat knew, first hand, how much Briley debated about her decision, but was glad she had taken the first step with Leah. "We've decided to see where things take us and if it leads to more, we're both okay with that."

"Kat, that's awesome. Now I know we need to get these envelopes right."

Kat leaned forward and buried her head in her hands. "I don't want to mess this up."

"Hey." Briley rubbed a hand up and down Kat's back. "You've got this. She already likes you."

"I know, but she's always telling me I'm too good to be true…and that's not the case at all. I can be a total screw up in relationships. I'm terrified." She was more than terrified; she was petrified. Dylan had swept into her life at a time that wasn't optimal, but she wouldn't change it for anything.

Briley looked thoughtful. "Have you told her that?"

"No." Kat straightened up and leaned back against the cushion, accepting Stripes when he climbed up her arm to settle on her shoulder.

"You should. I bet she's terrified too."

"You think?" The next time they talked, she would try and work up the nerve to bring it up. She didn't want to keep anything from Dylan, especially the way she was feeling. She prayed that she wouldn't stumble over her words. She always seemed to be a mess whenever Dylan was around. "So, how about we order dinner, then get started on our project?"

Briley grinned and stood, waving her hand at the boxes. "This is going to be awesome. I'm a little jealous that I didn't think of this. Leah would have loved it."

"You can do it now." Kat shrugged.

"Please." Briley shook her head. "She'll know I got the idea from you. I've got to up my wooing from here on out. I even downloaded Pinterest to my phone."

"You have Pinterest?" It was one app Briley said she would never download, even as crafty as she was.

It felt nice to be influencing Briley's wooing skills for once.

"I have to keep Leah on her toes."

Kat waved her hand in the air. "You're engaged, Briley. You've got her."

Briley pushed her glasses up the bridge of her nose and glared at Kat. "Just because we're engaged doesn't mean I'm going to stop surprising her or trying to woo her. No, now that she said yes, I'm going to do everything in my power to show her and the kids how much they mean to me. You've just shown me I can do more." She pointed at the boxes on the coffee table.

"Where will you find the time?" That was one of Kat's worries. Not having enough time to do everything. She pushed her limits as it was, especially with her accounting clients. Sooner than expected, she would have to let them go. The tiny house business ate up too much of her time to keep a second job.

"Kat, you make time. You set your priorities and stick with them. That's it. Could Brandon and I flip more houses? Of course, but then we'd be compromising on family time. When we first started our business, we devoted all our time to it, but once we hit a groove and met the right people, we were able to take a step back and assess everything. We both decided early on that family was important, but so was self-care. If we don't take care of ourselves, how are we supposed to be both physically and mentally healthy for anyone else? Also, Brandon and Mary are trying to have a baby."

Kat sat back and regarded Briley. When had her little sister grown up so much? "Wow. Maybe I should have been listening to you all along."

"I know, right?"

"I can see why Leah fell in love with you."

"Kat," Briley groaned.

"Just saying." Kat stood and drew Briley into a hug. "I love you."

"I love you too." She squeezed Kat's forearms and stood back. "Food."

"You know where the menus are."

"Any requests?"

"Nope. You choose."

Two hours later, and after they'd finished off their double pepperoni and cheese pizza, both were on the floor in front of the coffee table working on the envelopes. Kat had to admit Briley had a knack for it. The finished ones looked great. Almost Pinterest perfect.

"Wait a minute," Briley said. She held the glue gun in the right hand and a horse sticker in the other. "I thought you were making a scrapbook of Griffin's accomplishments, like the rest of us?"

"Oh." Kat bit her lip and adhered the star sticker onto an envelope. "Okay. The truth is I've been keeping everything in a shoe box."

"But," Briley spluttered. "I bought you a scrapbook and supplies."

"It's in my closet." Kat narrowed her eyes when Briley mumbled. "What was that?"

"I said, if I knew you weren't using it, I would have taken yours instead of buying another one."

"Another one?" Kat blinked. "You've already filled one up?"

"Two," Briley stated proudly. "She's my daughter. I don't want to miss anything. When she gets older, I want her to know how each of her accomplishments made me feel. No matter how small they were. I'm also keeping a journal of sorts of the events in Evan and

Madison's lives."

"You're amazing. They are all very lucky."

"I...yes, but I'm the lucky one. Extremely lucky." She sniffled.

"Bri, what's wrong?"

She set the glue gun and sticker on the table. "Sometimes it hits me how lucky I am. When I wake up in Leah's arms, or playing with Griffin, as well as spending time with Evan and talking with Madison. I'm so lucky, Kat. I'm terrified too, but they're worth it. Being with them is worth me worrying about Evan getting in with the wrong crowd, or Griffin getting hurt, or God forbid something happening to Leah, or Madison and her family. They will always be worth it, and I believe you're starting to feel a little bit of that too for Dylan and Emma."

Kat took a deep breath. "I am. I'm not ready to call it love yet, but I love spending time with them, and my thoughts are always on them."

"What you're feeling is normal. I feel it every day."

"You're right. Dylan and I promised to not rush things and live day to day."

"Day to day, huh?" Briley's grin set Kat on edge. "What did she say when you told her you were devoting the next year of your life to her and Emma?" She picked up the glue gun and continued with her envelope.

Kat opened and shut her mouth. Shit. That was exactly what she'd done. She'd planned the next year of their life together without even realizing it. With a groan, she dropped her head back to the couch. What was she thinking?

"Though, I wouldn't worry about it if I were you." With a flourish, Briley handed Kat the finished envelope.

"Why?" Kat slid the envelope into Emma's box.

"Well, Dylan did give the okay to all of your activities with Emma. That she trusts you with her daughter should tell you all you need to know. If the whole year thing bothered her, she would have told you. Dylan doesn't strike me as the type of woman who does what she doesn't want to. Am I right?"

That was true. Dylan hadn't commented on it, but like with her feelings, she would bring it up the next time they talked. "Yes, you're right. Let's get this done."

"Hell, yeah." Briley high-fived her. "By the way, next Tuesday night, I'm going to take Leah out. Can you watch Griffin?"

Kat frowned when the sticker wouldn't adhere to the envelope. "Evan can't?" She'd noticed that he was spending more time with his friends. It both delighted and made her sad.

"He's got a big test on Friday and needs to study." Briley cut her eyes to Kat. "Can you watch her? If not, that's fine. I can see if Ashley will."

Ashley was one of Briley's good friends. Even though Ashley was nice, Kat would never pass up the opportunity to spend time with her niece. "Sure. What time do you need me there?"

"Can you make it by six-thirty? We don't have any reservations anywhere. I just felt we needed a night out."

Kat went over her schedule in her mind. "Can we make it seven?"

"Sure." Briley plopped another envelope into Kat's hand. "I bet I can finish mine before you finish yours."

"You're on."

Three hours and a ton of snacks later, Briley had gone home after winning their competition. Kat stretched out on the couch staring at the finished envelopes. Those envelopes represented the next year of her life. A year she planned to willingly spend with Dylan and Emma. To anyone else it might not seem like a big deal, but to Kat it was everything. She hoped Dylan felt the same way.

Chapter Twenty

With a groan, Dylan stretched her back after she finished cleaning the bathroom in one of the hotel rooms. They'd had a busy day with almost twenty rooms apiece because one of the other housekeepers called in and she still had four rooms to go. Not to mention that two of her rooms were trashed and it had taken almost an hour to clean each one. She wouldn't be able to pick Emma up from school, so she'd called her mom to take care of it.

"Earth to Dylan." Dylan spun around, coming face to face with Haley, who looked as tired as she did.

"You okay?" Haley asked. "I'm asking because for the last few months you've practically had a smile plastered to your face and not the frown that is currently in its place. It doesn't seem to have anything to do with the long day we've had."

Dylan glanced at the clock and figured it was close enough to their break that they could go ahead and take it. "Just thinking about Kat."

Haley leaned back against the nearest wall. "Things not going well?"

"It's not that." Dylan bit her lip.

"You don't have to tell me, if you don't want to."

"I like her. A lot. But she seems too good to be true. You know? Says the right things. Does the right things. My daughter adores her, and they haven't even spent that much time together. I've never had a relationship like this before. It's strange. I try not to think about the other shoe dropping, but sometimes it's hard not to. Kat makes it so easy." She pulled her gloves off and ran her hand down her face.

Haley smiled and squeezed Dylan's shoulder. "I've been there before. Not sure if you should open up or if you should even take a chance. It's hard wondering if you should trust your heart or your head." Dylan nodded. That was exactly what she was feeling. "I'm not an expert on relationships but let me ask you something. When you're with her, what do you feel?" Haley held her hand up. "Don't think, just talk."

"Safe. Happy. Content." She buried her head in her hands and after a moment turned to look at Haley. "She's funny, smart, compassionate." Dylan smirked. "Sexy as hell."

"I know." Haley laughed. "How do you feel when she's interacting with Emma?"

"Like Emma couldn't be in safer hands." Dylan's eyes widened. "Oh, God."

"It's okay," Haley quickly said, and patted Dylan's hand.

"No." Dylan stood. "It's way too soon for that."

"Maybe, maybe not." Haley pushed away from the wall and took Dylan's hand. "Don't overthink this. You still have some reservations. Talk to her."

"I will. I wish we had more time together, but what time we do spend she's always so focused on us. Ian was great, but I never felt like this with him." Guilt was something she'd dealt with for the last couple of weeks. She knew it was unfounded, but it seemed to always be just on the surface. "For God's sake, we haven't even kissed yet."

Haley laughed. "That's easily remedied. As for

the guilt. Well, would Ian want you to be sad? He would want you to move on, wouldn't he?"

"He would. I know that." She shook her head and sighed. "I think I'm overthinking everything. My mom said I should go with the flow and I'm trying."

"Look." Haley grasped her shoulders. "I think it's time you had a heart to heart with her. Lay all your worries down and talk all this through. It's the only way you're going to be able to get over this."

"You're right. We're supposed to meet this weekend." She smiled, thinking about the envelopes Kat was going to give them on Saturday. They both agreed not to tell Emma beforehand. It would be a nice surprise and Dylan knew Emma would appreciate it. "Thank you, Haley."

"Any time." Haley glanced at the clock. "Back to work."

"Hopefully, these last rooms fly by."

The rest of the rooms took a couple of hours and then she was pulling into Miller's grocery store. It hit her earlier in the week that Kat put more into this relationship than she did, and it was time she stepped up. And, more than once, she received praise as a fantastic gift giver. Once inside, she picked up a basket and headed toward the candy aisle. She'd settled on a budget and had downloaded a few of the digital coupons the store offered this week to help with the final cost.

Her thoughts wandered as she picked up and threw several items into her basket. She knew Kat would appreciate anything Dylan gave her, but she wanted to make it special. After checking out, she headed across town to the pet store. Before she could talk herself out of it, she wandered inside and quickly located the aisle she was looking for. Five minutes later, she was still staring at the shelf.

"Looking for something?" A voice said to her right.

Dylan knew that voice, and slowly turned to look at Briley, who had a knowing look on her face. "Stripes."

Briley nodded and stepped up beside her, then touched an item. "That one is nice."

Dylan reached for and pulled the small hoodie off the peg. It was black and gray with a red stripe down the sides. It would go good with Stripes' coloring and it was only a couple of dollars higher than she budgeted for. "Thank you."

Briley fidgeted. "Look, I know we don't know each other that well, and while I hope that changes, you're not the priority in my life." Dylan flinched but kept quiet. "I love my sister and want what's best for her."

"I understand."

"I don't think you do. Kat is amazing and what you see is what you get. God," Briley groaned, "she'd get so upset with me for saying this, but it needs to be said."

"If it's something she should tell me, I would like to hear it from her." There was no way she wanted Briley to divulge Kat's secrets to her.

Briley nodded but plowed ahead. "Kat wears her heart on her sleeve, but she's not always good with letting her walls down. Don't run before you have a chance to knock a few of said walls down. Just give her time. Please don't hurt her without just cause."

"Briley, I would never do that. It's come to my attention today that there are things we need to discuss and the sooner the better. But I also realized that Kat has been giving more to this relationship than I have lately and that needs to change. I like your sister."

"She likes you too."

"I would hope so, as much time as we've been spending together."

"Good. Good." Briley tapped her cart that cat and dog food, along with a few toys filled. "I need to get going, but it was good to see you. I mean it about us getting together and baking." Briley dug into her purse and pulled out a pencil and piece of paper, scribbled something on it, then handed it to Dylan. "My number. If you're going to be spending more time with Kat, which it looks like at least the next year is locked in, you should have my number."

Dylan slipped the paper in her pocket. So, Briley knew about the envelopes as well. "Thank you and I should get going."

"Have a good rest of your day."

"I will."

After paying for her purchase, she headed home.

Five hours later, she still felt restless. Emma had gone to bed two hours ago, but Dylan couldn't get Kat off her mind and what they needed to talk about. When Kat had called at nine-thirty their nightly talk was short, but sweet, and Dylan hadn't worked up the nerve to delve into the talk they needed to have. She debated about calling Kat again, when her mother took the phone from her hands.

"You should go and talk to her."

"It's late."

"Honey, if you're this worked up over it, text her to let her know you need to talk, then go over there."

Her mom was right. "Let me have my phone."

Dylan: You up?
Kat: Yes.
A moment later her phone rang. "Hello."
"Everything okay?" Kat asked.
Dylan swung her legs over the couch and sat up. "Not really."
"What's wrong? Do I need to come over?"
"No, but would you mind if I came over to your place?" There was a long pause; Dylan worried that Kat had hung up.
"Sure. You can come over."
"I'll be there shortly."
"Okay."
Twenty minutes later, Dylan pulled into Kat's driveway and cut the engine. Before she even got out of the car, the front door opened, and Kat stepped out a few feet, dressed in a pair of plaid sleep pants and a white tank top. The worried look set Dylan in motion. "It's not bad, Kat. I promise."
Kat's features relaxed. She stepped back through the door so Dylan could enter. They both settled close together on the couch.
Dylan took Kat's right hand. "Really, it's nothing bad, but sometimes when I get something on my mind, I need to talk it out, no matter what time it is."
"You're welcome any time, Dylan."
"I have something to say…that I want you to know." Dylan stood and started pacing. "You're perfect. Always saying and doing the right things. It's so frustrating sometimes." She stopped pacing and fixed her gaze on Kat, who sat quietly on the couch with an unreadable expression. "I want so much to believe everything you say and do, and it would be so easy to. But there's this little voice in my mind that

won't let me forget that everything could fall apart in a moment's notice. Emma would be devastated, and frankly, so would I." She paused, then took a deep breath. "I know how you feel about me, but I'm not always great at expressing my feelings. I don't want you to feel like I'm not in this as much as you are." Another pause and deep breath. "I like you, Kat. A lot. And I find myself more scared than happy when I'm left alone with my thoughts. I don't like that feeling. You've done nothing for me to distrust you…yet it's still there." She stared at Kat, waiting for her to say something.

"I'm terrified." Kat stood. "I look at you and Emma and can see my future, but I'm shit at relationships. I either give too much or not enough. I miss birthdays, and holidays. I've always had walls up, but I find you easily knocking them down and it scares the hell out of me. I have just as much to lose as you do. If this doesn't work, I'm going to be devastated, and I've never felt that way about anyone before. In my past relationships, it's always been one day at a time." She closed her eyes for a moment and shook her head. "But fuck. I've planned the next year of my life with you and Emma in mind. Who does that, and you went with it? I hope you know you can tell me anything. I screw up, Dylan, all the time. I think we haven't spent enough time together for you to see that. I'm scared that when we do spend more time together, you'll see that I'm not perfect and not be interested anymore. I hate to think about a day when you don't want me in your life anymore."

"Kat, I'm terrified too, for a lot of the same reasons you are. You've mostly only seen the good side of Emma. You've never had to comfort her from a nightmare or hold her when she's cried herself to sleep. Our life isn't a picnic. As you know, I'm up to my eyeballs in debt with Emma's bills. I work my ass off, and it never feels like enough. She's disabled and it's not easy. She's not always happy. You could do so much better than me." Dylan swiped at her tears.

"I'm not scared of the hard times. I welcome them. It means we're growing and evolving. I want this relationship to go somewhere." She held Dylan's gaze, her voice sincere. "I can't promise I'll always understand, but I'll always be willing to listen and talk things through. Like now. This is hard. I don't want to mess up and I'm terrified I won't be enough for you or Emma. Yes, I have a healthy bank account, but I never want you to feel like you're not enough for me. You are and so is Emma. I don't care how much money you have, or how many jobs you work, or where you work. Do I want you working yourself to death?" She shook her head. "No, but I understand and I'm more than willing to help you find a job that will get you more financially secure, but only if that's something you want my help with. I like the way you look, but I'll be here to help if you decided you want to try and lose weight. I just want you healthy, and right now you are. I..." Kat ran a hand through her hair, leaving it standing straight up.

Before Dylan could think about her actions, she entered Kat's personal space and smoothed Kat's hair back down. She relaxed even more when Kat's arms slipped around her and pulled their bodies flush together.

"The hard times scare me. You scare me." Dylan rested her head on Kat's shoulder.

Kat rubbed her cheek against Dylan's hair. "And

that's okay. You scare me too. Emma scares me. I'll be here, though. I don't plan on going anywhere. I'm not a player. Far from it. You're the only woman I want." Kat pulled back enough to search Dylan's face. With one hand, she cupped Dylan's jaw.

"I'm nobody."

"You're somebody to me."

Dylan braced herself when Kat closed the distance between them. She trembled with the first touch of Kat's lips on hers. The kiss was over before it even started. She pulled Kat down into their second one. This one was more fervent. Dylan boldly slipped her tongue against Kat's lips, gently requesting entrance. Kat opened to her, their tongues lightly stroking, making Dylan feel a little dizzy. Not wanting to escalate the kiss into something more, Dylan gently bit Kat's bottom lip before she pulled away.

Dylan's voice was a little breathless. "Another thing I can add to the list that you're good at."

Kat looked a bit off balance. "So, I'm a list now?"

"Yes." Dylan slipped her arms around Kat's neck and stroked the hair on Kat's nape. It was softer than she thought it would be. "You mean more to me right now than I'm ready to admit. Just know, I'm here because I want to be, not because I feel like I should be."

"I know. We have things to work on, and I feel we're on the right track. I don't mind admitting I'm scared as long as you don't run because of it."

"I will never run when you're being honest with me. I don't want secrets between us. I want to be able to come to you with my hopes, and my fears," Dylan said.

Kat pecked her on the lips. "You mean more to

me than I'm willing to admit right now too."

Dylan pulled away and flopped down on the couch, pulling a willing Kat with her. "Can we cuddle?" It was the first time she'd ever tried to initiate anything physical with Kat, but she knew Kat would never laugh at or judge her for anything she wanted.

"Are you kidding? I am an ace cuddler." Kat leaned back on the couch and opened her left arm for Dylan to cuddle against her. Dylan obliged, liking the feel of Kat's arm holding her close as she sunk into the warmth that was Kat.

"Do you have a trophy for said cuddling?"

Kat let out an amused snort. "No, but I should."

"Well, considering I'm your girlfriend, it looks like the acquisition of said trophy will fall to me." Dylan closed her eyes as Kat's warmth immersed her in contentment.

"I couldn't have said it better myself." Kat kissed the top of her head and held her tighter.

Dylan spent the next hour with Kat. When home and in her bed, memories of Kat's kisses danced in her mind. The reality was so much better than her day dreams.

Chapter Twenty-one

With a yawn, Kat stretched before swinging her legs off the bed to stand. After she breezed through her morning routine, and ate breakfast, she spent the morning with Stripes. Today was the first day of what she deemed Operation Envelopes. Also, Dylan and Emma were expecting her for lunch. Last month, she'd presented the envelopes to them, and both seemed excited by the prospect. They were impressed by the envelopes, and Kat had to come clean and tell them Briley had been the driving force behind the decorations.

Even though she had spent the last few months getting to know them, today felt different. Probably because it was the beginning of the next year for all of them. Nerves had started the night before after her nightly talk with Dylan and hadn't let up since. This Saturday was the first she'd had off this month and she felt excited for what the day would bring. With Halloween less than a month away, she'd wanted to get started on activities with them both.

Over the past month, she and Dylan had kept a clear line of communication open, but Kat had a feeling Dylan was still holding herself back a little. The main priority right now was making sure Dylan felt secure in their relationship. Kat was terrified it would all blow up in their faces or Dylan would realize it would be best for them to just be friends after all.

Today was month one and she wanted to start off with something Emma was familiar with. Kat went back and forth but decided on an afternoon of painting with Emma. New places or activities would sometimes overwhelm Emma and Kat didn't want her to be uncomfortable. Her feelings for Emma were as deep as those for Dylan. She wanted to make sure Emma knew that. Thinking that, in the future, Emma could consider her a mother figure was awe inducing.

Tonight, she was taking Dylan out for their first dinner date. Dylan had looked skeptical when she held her first envelope and saw the rainbow on the cover. She became even more stumped after opening it to reveal the word 'dinner.' Emma had figured out the location was at the riverfront where a twenty-foot-tall and eighty feet long rainbow sculpture had recently been installed.

The plan was to finish up with Emma around five, rush home, shower, and change, then be back by six-thirty to pick Dylan up. With the help of Briley and Leah, she'd chosen what she hoped was the perfect outfit. She might not have Briley's moves, but she could treat a woman to a fun night out and look good doing it. The day before, Kat had Lucille, her Corvette Stingray, detailed for their date.

After wiping off the kitchen counter, she turned on the radio, then danced into the living room. The workout that morning had done nothing to calm her nerves, so she needed to burn off some energy. She lifted Stripes off the floor, fell onto the couch, then cuddled him on her chest. "Is this what it feels like to be happy, Stripes?"

"It's exactly what it feels like."

Kat almost jumped off the couch, startling

Stripes. "Shit, Briley. You can't keep coming in here like that."

"Says who?" Briley settled into the chair across from the couch. "You're the one that gave me a key."

"Says me...and that was just for emergencies." Kat closed her eyes and relaxed to bring her breathing back to even.

"Are you excited for today?"

Kat popped one eye open. "So excited."

With a grin, Briley lifted her phone to snap a picture. "You two look adorable."

"Of course."

"So," Briley said after a moment.

Kat sat up, lifting her legs to the coffee table. "What did you bring?"

"Here." Briley thrust it into Kat's hands. "I made you some shortbread cookies to take with you."

"Thanks, Bri. You're my favorite sister." Shortbread was her favorite. "You know I don't have to exercise as much since I moved out of your house." She plopped a piece of a cookie into her mouth.

"At least I'm something," Briley mumbled. She shook her finger at Kat. "Please, you miss living with me."

"Only occasionally."

"Sure." They both sat quietly, comfortable in the silence. "You're taking Dylan to Mario's, aren't you?"

Kat set the cookies aside. "I've had the reservation for a month. You did recommend it."

"I've taken Leah there a few times. We both enjoyed it. Nice atmosphere, fantastic food, plus you can take a walk by the floodwalls and look at the murals afterward."

"That's the plan, plus the new sculptures that

were put in."

"Sounds good." Briley stood. "Don't forget we won't be here next weekend."

Kat rolled her eyes. This was about the tenth time Briley had reminded her. Over Christmas, Briley had gotten to know Madison, Leah's daughter, and her family, but was still nervous about spending time with them. "I know, Bri. You're going camping. Madison likes you; you don't have to be worried." Kat walked over to Briley. "You know something?"

"What?" Briley nervously bit on a thumbnail.

"Being with Leah has been good for you. Getting to know her kids has been good for you. Falling in love and becoming a mother has done wonders for you."

"Don't I know it. Well, I had better get going." Briley walked to the front door, then leaned against it. "Have fun and don't do anything I wouldn't do."

"Get out."

Kat shut the door on a laughing Briley. She couldn't help the smile that broke out. Today was going to be a good day.

An hour later, she gave herself a mini pep talk before heading to Dylan's house. Iris was spending the day shopping before she came back to watch Emma while they went out to dinner.

Her stomach flopped as she pulled into the drive and saw the living room curtains move. This wasn't the first time she'd visited here, but it felt different. When the front door opened, Emma walked out and waved. This put Kat's nerves to rest. She grabbed the box of supplies she'd bought and exited the truck. With a short pause, she took in the scene in front of her. Dylan stood behind Emma, wearing an apron and a dishtowel thrown over her shoulder. *Wow, sexy and all mine. Deep breath, Kat.*

Emma gave her a tight hug when she stepped onto the porch. Kat kissed the top of her head, then set the box on the swing to wrap her up in a proper hug.

"Emma, go wash up. Lunch is ready," Dylan said.

"Okay, Mom." Emma left to do as instructed.

Dylan stepped forward and grabbed the lapels of Kat's button-down to pull her forward until they were a breath apart. Kat placed her hands on Dylan's hips and leaned forward and kissed her.

"You can kiss later," Emma called out from behind them. "I'm hungry."

Kat smiled into the kiss before pulling back. "She's hungry."

Dylan drew her into a warm embrace. Dylan wasn't often snuggly, and Kat missed the contact as soon as Dylan pulled away.

"Let's eat," Dylan said.

Kat picked the box up and followed Dylan into the house.

"Put the box on the couch, then come to the table," Dylan instructed.

Once they were seated, Kat picked up her glass of water and held it up. "A toast." Dylan and Emma followed suit. "To having fun today."

"Having fun," Emma chimed.

"To fun," Dylan said.

Kat noticed the smirk on Dylan's oh so kissable lips and felt a rush of heat to her face. She quickly dove into eating her chicken salad sandwich.

"So, Kat," Emma said. "What did you bring?"

"Painting supplies. I bought a few canvases and thought we could go crazy with them. We can hang one up here and I can hang one up at work to brighten the place up. It'll be fun."

"That will be fun. Have you ever painted before?"

"Nope, but you have, and I'll just follow your lead."

"I can do that." Emma looked subdued, her expression a bit sad.

After they finished their lunch, Emma went into the living room to get everything ready. Kat pulled Dylan to a stop when she was clearing the table.

"You okay?" Dylan slipped her arms around Kat and pulled her close.

"She doesn't hate what we have planned, does she?"

"No, she doesn't. She's a little sad that Dad had to cancel their fishing trip next weekend. That's all. Once you two get started, she'll talk your ear off."

"Good. I want her to feel comfortable with me." She sank into the warmth of Dylan's arms about her.

"She is, but the more time you two spend together you'll see how relaxed she really is."

"I can't wait."

"I can't either. I'm glad you're here, Kat."

"I am too." She had a feeling today was going to be great.

Chapter Twenty-two

Dylan looked in the bedroom mirror, smoothed her hands over her stomach, and debated for the tenth time about the dress she'd chosen. Kat had said dress nice, but not fancy, though their definitions of the words could be different. The blue striped, sleeveless fit and flare dress fit that description, but maybe it was too simple. This was one reason why she didn't date much. Not just because of the time involved, but all the other details. Was it enough? Not enough? Should her hair be up or down? She huffed and turned away from the mirror, gasping at her mom standing by her door.

"You look beautiful, honey."

"It's..."

"Hush." Iris grasped Dylan's hands. "You look beautiful and Kat will be blown away. You deserve to be happy."

"I'm scared, Mom. What Ian and I had was nice. Comfortable, but what I feel for Kat keeps me awake at night and has me thinking long term." She squeezed Iris's hands. "Does that make me a bad person?"

"What? No. Come here." Iris patted the bed beside her for Dylan to sit. "What you and Ian had was real and you loved each other. What you feel for Kat will never diminish that or your relationship with him. Don't compare Kat to Ian or Ian to Kat; you won't like the outcome and you'll always be judging Kat by something that's not her fault. I like Kat, but I'm still skeptical about her, as I am Harold."

Dylan laughed. Her mom and Macy's husband still didn't get along all that well, but they were always cordial to each other and Macy and Harold had been married for fifteen years.

"But," Iris said. "If you're still having doubts about being with her, you need to make a decision soon. There is no need to string you both along."

"I'm not having doubts, per se. I guess." Dylan huffed and stood. "I guess I feel like I'm free-falling without a net, and I'm okay with that." She laughed. "That's crazy, right?"

"Oh, honey," Iris stood, "it's not crazy. It's love."

"It's too soon for that. For God's sake, she hasn't even had to sit through one of Macy and Harold's cookouts yet."

"She will in a couple of weeks."

Dylan wrung her hands. "But it hasn't been that long."

"You've known her for almost six months. I want you to be honest with me and honest with yourself, Dylan. Even since the beginning, she's never just been your friend. Your relationship with her has always been more than that for you."

Dylan turned from her mom and walked up to the window and stared out. She was lying to herself if she thought Kat had only ever been her friend. It had always been more. She braced her hands on the windowsill, taking a few deep breaths to calm her racing heart. How had Kat wiggled herself into her heart so soon? Without her even noticing? "It all feels like a dream and I'm afraid it's going to turn into a nightmare."

"I loved your father for a long time. Did I go into the relationship expecting to get divorced? Of course not, and you shouldn't go into this looking for it to fail. What kind of start is that?"

"But you did get divorced."

"Your father and I had our issues. You know this, but if given the chance, I would do it all the same again. It was worth it."

"Getting hurt was worth it?"

"It wasn't all hurting, Dylan. We had fun together, and we had you, but we grew apart. Some couples do. I'm not going to lie and say you and Kat will be forever, but dooming this relationship before it even gets started is going to kill it faster than anything else you could do." Iris cupped Dylan's cheeks. "You deserve this. Please allow yourself to love her. You've been holding back with her and you still fell in love and you feel like this. Just imagine if you would open yourself up to her and looked at this as if it was a dream and not a nightmare. You'd be floating on air."

Iris was right, but most of the time she was. Dylan reached for and grasped her Mom's hand when she saw Kat's car pull into the driveway.

"Would you look at that," Iris said. "I didn't even know she owned a car. I've only ever seen her in the truck. Looks like she's pulling out all the stops for you."

Dylan held back a snicker and felt her heart grow a little lighter when Kat stepped out of the car and looked to be giving herself a pep talk, if the waving of her hands was any indication.

"She cleans up nicely too," Iris said, then kissed Dylan on the cheek and walked out of the room.

Kat wore a pair of dark blue ankle length trousers, with a gray button-down with the first few buttons undone, and a pale blue sweater was tied loosely around her neck. She wore a pair of white boat shoes. Dylan's heart jumped when Kat reached into the car and pulled out a bouquet of flowers. Roses. Red. There was no way Kat didn't know the meaning of them, true love, and even though she hadn't verbally said the words they both knew what kind of statement Kat was making. It made everything fall into place, seeing the nervousness on Kat's features. At least they were in the same boat.

Thank God, Kat wouldn't be able to see her from her vantage point. She didn't want to look like a creeper. At the knock on the door, she turned her head and watched Emma walk into the room.

"Wow, Mom, you look nice," Emma said.

"You think so?" Dylan turned in a circle, showing off her dress.

"I like your dress."

With one final look in the mirror, Dylan took a deep breath and followed Emma, only for her to stop her at the bedroom door. "Emma?"

"I like her. Grams and I want you to be happy. It's okay to be happy. Dad wouldn't be mad."

Dylan bit back a sob and swept Emma into a hug. "He wouldn't, would he?"

"Nope. Unless everything you've told me about him has been a lie."

"Never." She kissed the top of Emma's head, then walked back to the mirror to check her make-up.

"Don't keep her waiting," Emma said, then left.

Why did this night feel so different?

Her feet took her down the hallway of their own accord and when she stepped into the living room, Kat and Iris stopped talking and turned to her.

"Wow. You look amazing," Kat said with a huge

grin, her eyes bright.

Dylan reached for the flowers, which Kat handed over.

"These are for you."

"I would hope so, and you hadn't decided to woo my mother instead." The flush to Kat's cheeks was always a welcome sight.

"Never," was Kat's answer.

"They're beautiful. Let me put them in some water then we can go."

"Sure thing." Kat put her hands in her pockets and rocked back on her heels.

Dylan reached forward with her free hand and smoothed the collar of Kat's shirt. "I'll be right back."

"I'm not going anywhere without you."

After filling a vase with water and putting the flowers in it, Dylan said goodnight to Emma and Iris, then followed Kat out to the car. She was charmed when Kat opened the passenger door for her. As soon as Kat was seated and turned to her, Dylan leaned forward and connected their lips. Not wanting to get carried away, she drew back after a few seconds.

"You look beautiful as well," Dylan said.

Kat opened her eyes and touched her lips. "Thank you." Kat's cheeks pinked, and her smile looked a bit shy. "Are you ready for tonight?"

"Woo me, Kat."

Kat's laugh as they pulled out of the driveway warmed her heart. Nothing was guaranteed, she knew that to be a fact, and the last thing she wanted to do was jinx this as it was just getting started. She placed her hand on Kat's leg and the smile she got in return was worth everything.

Forty minutes later they were seated at the

restaurant.

"Have you been here before?" Dylan asked, then lifted her wine glass and took a sip. The restaurant hadn't been at all what Dylan was expecting, but she loved Italian food and was glad Kat picked a moderately priced place for their first date.

"No. Briley recommended it." Kat nervously rolled up one edge of her napkin. "Is it all right?"

"It's great."

Conversation was easy and allowed dinner to progress nicely. After turning down dessert, Kat paid, and they were soon walking along the boardwalk beside the rainbow sculpture.

"It's a beautiful night," Kat said.

"I agree." Dylan tightened her hold around Kat's arm and allowed her to lead them toward an empty bench where they sat.

"I've had a good time tonight."

"I have too. You do know how to show a girl a good night." Dylan's chest warmed at the blush that raced up Kat's neck and into her face. She shivered when Kat held open her cardigan sweater and helped Dylan into it. "Thank you." Dylan smiled when Kat leaned forward and rested her forearms on her knees. "Something on your mind?" She placed her hand on Kat's back and stroked in circles.

"Only good things, I assure you."

Kat's smile made her feel lighter than she had in a long time. Her mom was right. She couldn't think about this being doomed before it even started. She stood from the bench so suddenly Kat looked up, startled, but accepted the hand Dylan reached toward her.

"My lady," Kat said, kissing the back of her hand.

Dylan pulled Kat flush against her, then ran her hands down Kat's shoulders and laced their fingers together. "Let's see if we can get someone to take our picture by the end of the rainbow."

"I think that's the best idea I've heard all day."

Dylan didn't even try to censor her smile as she watched Kat wrangle up a passing young woman to take their picture. She gladly handed over her phone to the woman, then relaxed back against Kat for the picture. As Kat's arms circled her waist, Dylan had never felt safer, and for the first time in months, she decided to put the doubts aside and enjoy the beginning of her own fairy tale in the making.

Chapter Twenty-three

Kat grunted as she held the top cabinet up while Kyle screwed it into place. Her arms screamed in pain, but she held steady while he made sure it was level. She'd already intensified her workouts once, and it looked like she'd have to do it again in order to stay in tip top shape.

"All good, boss?"

She ran her hand along the cabinet that Kyle had made from the reclaimed wood they'd brought home from the downed barn. "They're beautiful, Kyle. You have a way with the wood."

"Thanks. I like making something out of nothing." He snapped his fingers and drew Kat's attention back to him. "Speaking of. I got started on that dollhouse you wanted me to make for your kid for Christmas. It's looking good."

Kat didn't correct him about Emma being her kid because he would make the same mistake again. A few weeks ago, she'd asked him if he could build her a superhero inspired dollhouse, so Emma could put her Lego figures in it. "Thanks, man."

"No problem. It's going to be cool. Just you wait. I'll have it done for her by Christmas."

"I really appreciate it."

He waved off her words. "If it wasn't for you, I would still be living in my car."

"You would have found a way," Kat said.

He shrugged. "Maybe, maybe not, but I'm here now, and you shouldn't be."

"What?"

"Aren't you having lunch with Dylan?"

She glanced at her watch, then at her clothes, realizing she didn't have time to change if she wanted to make it in time. "Shit."

"I don't think she's going to complain about the tank top, boss." Kyle whistled, walking off.

After wiping off in the bathroom, she was resigned to still looking like she'd been working outside all day. She climbed into her truck and made her way to Dylan's work. She made a mental note to keep a button down in her truck for when she had lunch with Dylan. It wasn't usually an issue, but before hanging the cabinets, she and Reeva cleared their extra materials, which made her clothes filthy.

Kat tried not to think about the cookout Dylan had invited her to on Saturday. She'd been worrying about it all week and it was only Wednesday. In the six months that she'd known Dylan, she had never officially met her cousin Macy. Dylan had reassured her countless times, but it was still nerve-racking. Especially the way Iris talked about Harold. It made Kat wonder about what Iris thought of her.

Before her thoughts could sink any further, she pulled into the parking lot and climbed out of the truck. The looks directed her way as she walked through the lobby had her second guessing the decision to not go home and change clothes. When she entered the breakroom, the three women and one man seated there stared at her.

Haley motioned her forward, and the longer she

stared, the more Kat became uneasy.

"Sorry about the shirt."

"No need to apologize." She swept her eyes up Kat's body. "It's a nice tank top."

"Is Dylan around?" Kat stuffed her hands in her pockets. As much as she liked Haley, she wasn't there to see her.

Haley snickered. "Come with me." A few minutes later, Haley pointed to a room and took her leave.

"Hey."

A smile split her face and she slowly turned toward Dylan, who was biting her lip, even as her eyes raked down her body.

"Hi." Why did she always become tongue tied around this woman? She relaxed when Dylan ran her hand along her arm and grasped her bicep before pulling her along.

"We can eat in here." Dylan pulled her into the room.

"I tried to apologize for my tank."

Dylan shut the door, then pushed Kat up against the wall and ran her hands up her chest. "It's not the dirt, honey. It's your muscles. They're distracting."

"Oh." It was the first time Dylan had called her anything other than Kat and she liked it.

With a chuckle, Dylan leaned forward and slipped her hands behind Kat's neck. "Yes, 'oh.' You look enticing."

"I'm dirty."

"You're ripped." She briefly touched the tip of her tongue to her top lip, then pulled Kat down into a kiss.

Kat deepened the kiss and pulled Dylan even closer, their tongues dancing. Lately, their kisses had become heated. Kat pulled back and nipped Dylan's jaw. "We need to stop."

"How can I when you're so hot?"

Kat rubbed her nose against Dylan's. "You're so sexy you invade all my dreams. Trust me, I know how hard it is to keep my hands from roaming every inch of your body every time I see you. But, I don't want to be caught with my pants down."

Dylan groaned. "Do you always have to be so reasonable?"

"It's my curse."

"Smartass." Dylan smirked, then stepped away. "Food?"

"You bet."

"You wait here, and I'll go out and get it."

"Sounds good." Kat accepted the sheet Dylan handed her, threw it over the couch then sat and relaxed while Dylan retrieved their lunch. Work was as busy as usual, but it wasn't as hard as she thought to make time for Dylan and Emma. In fact, it was a must. Somehow, she'd kept from neglecting any of her family, but she knew that wouldn't always be the case. November was looking like a particularly jam-packed month. It would be a balancing act juggling everything she needed to. She hoped everyone understood. Especially Dylan and Emma. She'd already scheduled in the next to last Saturday of the month for their monthly date. First though, they had to get through October and Halloween.

"What has you so deep in thought?"

Kat made to get up, but Dylan waved her off then plopped down beside her, handing over a turkey sandwich and fruit cup.

"I hope this is okay."

Kat pecked her on the lips. "Looks good." After swallowing a large bite of sandwich, she took a sip of water. "Yum. Delicious." She sighed. "November is going to be a packed month for me. I have our date night planned, but if I want the week before Christmas free, I'll need to work almost every day until then. Including most Thursdays. At least, that's what it looks like now. I'm hoping we can finish before that, but it's not looking good." She took another bite and waited for Dylan to say something.

"What are you scared to tell me?" Dylan frowned. "We don't own you, Kat. I don't expect you to spend all your time with us and I can easily bring you lunch at work. I mean, you have to eat."

"See, that's the thing, I'm not scared, but apprehensive. I want to spend all my time with you and Emma. We officially started dating and I don't want you to feel like I'm neglecting you two. I know Emma will be disappointed."

Dylan cupped Kat's cheeks. "Listen carefully." Kat nodded. "We want to spend all our time with you too, but right now that's not realistic. I know you're not a workaholic, but I also know you recently started this business. I want it to be successful, and frankly I'm surprised you were able to spend as much time with us as you have the last few months. It brought us to this point, but I'm not mad. You're a hard worker. Don't ever be scared to talk to me." She kissed her lightly on the lips.

"Now who's saying all the right things? My girlfriends in the past haven't always been so receptive to my working habits."

"I'm not them."

"Thank God for that."

They finished the rest of their lunch in silence and once their trash was thrown away, they cuddled on the couch. "How long do you have left?" Kat asked.

"Ten minutes." Dylan relaxed into Kat's side. "So—" The ringing of Kat's phone interrupted her.

"It's just Briley. It can wait." But when it stopped ringing it started up again.

"Kat, answer your phone."

Kat swiped at the screen then raised the phone to her ear. "This better be important, Briley."

"It is."

"So?"

"Are you sitting down?"

The tone of Briley's voice threw her off. "Is Griffin okay? Leah? Evan?" Dylan gripped Kat's arm.

Briley hurried on. "They're fine."

"Then why do you sound like someone died?"

A beat later. "Mom's here."

Kat pulled the phone away from her ear then brought it back. "I'm sorry, what?"

"You heard me."

"It sounded like you said Mom's here."

"She is."

Kat's eyes widened. "When you say here, you mean—?"

"She's sitting on the couch, Kat. Get your ass over here now."

"Where are you? And I have to go back to work."

"I'm in my kitchen. Get here now."

Briley ended the call. Kat slumped back on the couch, pressing her hands over her eyes. "Fuck."

"So, your mom's here." Dylan ran her fingers along Kat's stomach.

Kat slowly turned and groaned at the twinkle in

Dylan's eyes. Kat had already explained her mom to Dylan early in their relationship. She loved her mom, but they didn't always get along. They hadn't seen her in two years. "Briley's house." She wiped a hand across her brow. "Oh, man. Briley was hiding in the kitchen."

"Babe, it will be okay." Dylan kissed her, then pulled her up, handed her a brownie, pushed her out of the room, escorted her to the lobby doors and outside.

"I'll talk to you later."

Dylan grinned. "It's a date."

Forty minutes later, Kat pulled into her driveway and cut the engine. In the rearview mirror, her eyes locked onto Briley and their mom sitting on the swing on Briley's front porch. Calling forth confidence from the pit of her soul, she made her way across the street and bounded up the steps to the house.

"Mom."

"Katherine."

Their mom was the only person that called her that, but Kat didn't mind. It always seemed like something special between them. Her mom's hair was a little longer and curled around her shoulders. There were a few more wrinkles on her face, and a bit more grey in her hair, but she was still beautiful, and she looked happy. The last time she saw her mom she'd looked so stressed. It was nice to see her look more carefree.

Kat stepped forward and engulfed her mom in a hug that was readily accepted. Chanel number five would always be her favorite fragrance because it was what her mom always wore. She kissed her on the cheek then stepped back and leaned against the railing. She didn't realize until this moment how much she had missed her, and she wasn't sure what to do with her swirling feelings.

"I like the haircut," Deborah Anderson said.

"Thanks, Mom." Kat looked to Briley, who looked to have calmed down since her phone call.

"So, what brings you here?" Kat asked while Briley fidgeted with the hem of her t-shirt.

"That's what I wanted to talk to you both about." She patted Briley on the knee. "I've been going to therapy for the last six months and I've come to realize a few things." She held up her hands, palms out. "Please don't interrupt me." They both nodded. "After your father's death, I didn't treat either of you fairly. I became depressed and took it out on the both of you and for that I'm sorry."

Kat shared a look with Briley but they both kept their mouths shut. It wasn't like their mom to offer up an apology freely.

"The time I've missed of your lives is something I can never have back, but I'm here now and I hope that we can try again." Deborah audibly swallowed. "I love you both so much and I treated you so poorly. When Briley told me she was getting married, it hit me how much time I had let slip past us. I'm not sure you need a mother now, but I was at least hoping we can be friends." She stood and touched both their arms. "I'm going to get a cup of coffee; please talk things through and let me know what you decide."

As she walked off, Kat blurted out, "Mom, stop." From the set of her mother's shoulders, Kat already knew what she thought their answer would be, but she wasn't the only one that had changed. "Mom, I do blame you, especially how we were treated in our younger years, but I could have made more of an effort when I grew up and moved away and I didn't. I let my anger for how you treated us keep me away. I'm sorry." She saw the way Dylan and Iris interacted and even though she may never have that type of relationship with her mom, she was at a place that she wanted to try. Seeing the tears in her mom's eyes was almost her undoing.

"Kat's right," Briley said. "I resented you for a long time and could never understand why you always chose to stay away from us. I would have loved to have you here for this past Christmas but I'm willing to try if you are, but it must be a two-way street and I have a family now. Griffin gets attached easily and I don't want her falling in love with you, then you abruptly leaving. It wouldn't be fair to anyone."

Kat slipped her arm around Briley's shoulders and pulled her flush against her side. "Bri's right. My girlfriend has a seven-year-old daughter who also gets attached easily. I won't introduce you to them unless you promise not to disappear."

"I promise. You two have become amazing women." When she was close to them, Kat drew her into a group hug.

"We love you, Mom."

"I love you too."

Chapter Twenty-four

Dylan hummed and stirred the sauce that was bubbling on the stove. A quick glance at the clock hanging above the fridge let her know that Macy and Harold would be there in less than thirty minutes. She'd been a little disappointed when Kat had called and cancelled their dinner plans so she and Briley could have dinner with their mom. She had reassured Kat she wasn't mad, and she hoped they had a good time and settled things between them.

That had freed up her night. Iris had quickly called Macy and she'd agreed to come for dinner.

She knew Kat was nervous about the upcoming cookout and planned to take some time to talk with Macy about it tonight. There was a difference with Kat being uncomfortable about meeting them and Macy and Harold deliberately making Kat uncomfortable with their questioning.

"Mom, it smells so good." Emma stepped up next to her.

"Want a taste?"

"Yes, please." Dylan scooped up a small amount and had Emma blow on it a few times before allowing her to eat it.

"What do you think?"

"More garlic."

"Your wish is my command." Dylan added more garlic and after getting Emma's seal of approval, turned the burner down to simmer and put the lid on the pot. She leaned back against the counter and regarded Emma, who was standing by the table. Her little girl was growing up so fast. "Something on your mind, sweetie?" She brushed the hair out of Emma's eyes. It looked like a haircut was in order.

"Are we still going to visit Gramma and Grandpa before Christmas?"

"Come here." Dylan lead Emma to the couch and once she was seated, pulled Emma down and flush against her side. Ever since she was little, Emma didn't like to have emotional talks face to face, and if Emma was willing to talk, Dylan didn't mind. "Of course. What brought this on?"

"You're dating Kat now, and she has a family and I wasn't sure if that would mean I wouldn't see them anymore." Emma rested her head back against Dylan's chest.

"Sweetie, just because your dad isn't here anymore and just because I'm dating Kat, doesn't mean I wouldn't let you spend time with your grandparents. They will always be your grandparents just like Ian will always be your dad. Nothing will ever change that." She'd talked to Brett and Diane, Ian's parents, when she and Kat decided to start dating and, although supportive, they were hesitant to give their blessing. They were of course concerned for Emma, but Dylan had reassured them Emma's feelings would always be her priority. Their relationship was strained at times, but they loved Emma, and Dylan respected that.

Dylan held Emma tighter. "Emma, I would never keep you from spending time with them. They love you so much and are looking forward to spending time with you. You can always come to me with your concerns. As long as you want to spend time with them you can."

"I'm glad. I love them too."

"Just because I'm dating Kat doesn't mean the people in our lives are going to disappear. It just means we're expanding the people in our lives. You like Kat, right?"

"I do. A lot." Emma nodded.

Dylan breathed a sigh of relief. "She likes you too. What about Briley and Leah and their kids? You like them too, don't you?"

"Yes." She held tightly to Dylan's arm. "Change can be hard."

"Yes, sweetie, it can be. I know things have changed, but I never want you to feel like I'm neglecting you. If, for some reason, you feel like we're not getting enough one on one time, let me know. You'll always be my number one."

"I like that you spend time with Kat. She loves us."

"I do believe she does."

"I love her."

"Yeah?" Dylan couldn't help her pleased smile.

"Yeah."

"Well," Dylan said. "the next time we see her, you should tell her. I'm sure she would love that."

"I will."

"Just because your dad isn't alive anymore doesn't mean that his family isn't still a part of yours. They always will be."

"And yours."

"And mine." She kissed Emma on the top of her head. "Feel better?"

"You always make me feel better."

Dylan looked to the kitchen when her mom motioned to her.

"Macy and Harold just pulled up," Iris said.

Dylan moved so she could look Emma in the eye and held up her hand. "Ready for this?"

Emma smiled and slapped Dylan's hand with hers. "Yup."

Fifteen minutes later, after hugs and greetings, everyone was seated around the table, eating homemade pasta and sauce.

"So," Macy said, after taking a sip of her wine. "No Kat tonight. I'll admit to being a little curious of her, considering I haven't even met her properly yet."

"Nope," Emma said. "She's having dinner with her mom, but she's great." She twirled the noodles on her fork and took a big bite.

"Really?" Macy arched her brow. "You like her?"

Emma swallowed then took a sip of her juice. "Nope. I love her."

Macy looked from Emma to Dylan. "And does she love you?"

"Macy." Iris warned.

"Mom, it's all right," Dylan said. She knew Macy would do this and knew she was just looking out for them. "Yes, she loves us." She waited for the next question and didn't have to wait long.

"She's told you that?" Macy questioned.

Dylan set her napkin on the table and let a smile grace her lips. "No, but love isn't only about words. It's in the way she acts with us and the way she treats Emma and Mom. The way she treats me. I've never felt so cared for before or never felt so safe than when I'm with her. I trust her with Emma." She looked at her mom, then back to Macy. "And I trust her with my heart."

"I'm happy for you, Dylan," Harold said, after patting her hand.

He was a good man and Dylan still wasn't sure why her mom still gave him a hard time. He loved Macy and treated her like a queen and that was all that mattered to Dylan. "You'll meet her this weekend and please don't give her the third degree. She's already nervous enough as it is."

"You don't want me to talk to her?" Macy asked, but Dylan knew from the tone she wasn't happy about that.

"I don't have any problem with you talking to her, but please wait to interrogate her when there aren't so many people around. I don't want her to feel uncomfortable."

Macy sat back and crossed her arms. "I thought you said she was confident."

"She is, but she doesn't deserve the third degree from you. I don't need you to approve. Mom does and so does Emma, and right now that's good enough for me."

Macy shot Iris a look. "You approve of her?"

Iris nodded. "Yes. She's good for Dylan and if you would take a second to consider your cousin instead of yourself, you will see that she even looks lighter. Kat makes them both happy and I approve of that, like I approve of Harold making you happy. That being said, I still have my reservations about him as I probably always will, and the same goes for Kat. That doesn't mean I wouldn't be there for either of them in a heartbeat, but you two and Emma will always be my main priority."

Macy deflated before their eyes. "Aunt Iris

is right; you do look like a weight has been lifted. I promise I'll behave at the cookout."

"Good. Macy, I want you to like her, but it's not a requirement for me continuing to see her."

"Fair enough. I'm only looking out for your best interests."

"And I love you for it."

The silence stretched on, then Emma spoke up. "What's for dessert?"

Dylan watched in amusement as Harold jumped up, pulled Emma's chair out then escorted her to the refrigerator and showed her what they'd brought.

Macy looked at Harold and Emma, then turned back to Dylan and leaned forward on the table, lowering her voice. "I liked Ian, I thought he was good for you, but I never saw you look as carefree as you do right now. I'm really happy for you, Dylan."

Dylan bit her lip. "I loved Ian, but I've never felt like this and it's scary. So scary. I don't want to screw this up."

"You will at some point but screwing up doesn't mean an end. I screw up all the time, as does Harold, but we're both all in and fight to keep what we've got going. If she's all in like you are, I won't have a problem with her. Fights happen. Disagreements happen. We've both slept on the couch or in the guest room at some point and that's okay. I wouldn't want to make this journey without him."

"It shows. I really like her, Macy. Like." She shot her hands up and out, fingers spread wide. "Ka-boom!"

Macy laughed. "It feels good, huh?"

"It feels fantastic."

Chapter Twenty-five

Kat had just come downstairs when her front door opened and Briley walked in. They'd talked the night before about their mom being back and although they both wanted to give their relationship with her another chance, it was still unnerving that their mom had made such a turn around.

"Bri, everything all right?"

Briley paced in front of the front door. "She's so nice." Briley groaned. "And she wants to know about me. It's weird, Kat."

"I know." Kat joined her on the couch. Since Briley was the one with kids, their mom stayed at her house. If that hadn't been the case, Kat was sure that their mom would have stayed with her.

"No, you don't. I chickened out last night and went to bed early, leaving Leah to deal with her." Briley nervously tapped her right thumb against the tips of her fingers.

"You can't be serious. Leah doesn't even know her."

"I know." Briley groaned. "Leah's already informed me I owe her a month of top-notch wooing to make up for it. It's not like I left them to talk all night. Leah came to bed about an hour after I did. She wouldn't tell me what they talked about. Only that they were both amicable toward each other." Briley grimaced. "I feel like such a shit fiancée."

Kat laughed. "I wouldn't go that far. It's not like they hadn't talked any yesterday. Maybe it was good for them to get to know each other."

"Leah is great."

The dreamy look in Briley's eyes used to make her envious, but she had a feeling she looked the same way when thinking about Dylan. "Is everyone ready for breakfast?"

"Should be." Briley looked over her shoulder. "I snuck out to come over here. Evan spent the night at a friend's, so he won't be joining us."

"Well," Kat said. "Let's get going."

Forty minutes later, Kat, Briley, Leah, Griffin, and Deborah were seated around a table at the Wanderer, a restaurant prized for their made from scratch waffles and in-house made sausage.

"Aunt Kat."

Kat looked up from her menu and tugged Griffin into her lap.

"You spoil her, Kat," Leah said, but there was no bite in her words.

"It is my prerogative, is it not?"

"That's what you've been telling us." Briley placed an arm across the back of Leah's chair.

"So, girls," Deborah said. "What do you recommend?"

Kat opened her mouth, but Briley beat her to it. "Can't go wrong with the waffle and sausage. Or for something lighter, the Greek yogurt parfait is good. Leah usually always gets their egg white omelet. Evan always gets the pecan pancakes with strawberries and whipped cream. Really can't go wrong with anything."

After their orders were taken, Kat plopped Griffin back in her booster seat with a bop on the nose then turned to her mom. "So, Mom, how long do you plan on staying?"

"I hadn't really thought about it, but I would like to stay until the wedding, at least."

That was less than a year away. A part of Kat, the doubting part, settled a little at her mom's declaration. She knew Deborah couldn't stay with Briley that long and wasn't a hundred percent sure she wanted her to stay with her, but there wasn't any reason not to offer. "If you need somewhere to stay, you can stay with me." The look on Briley's face almost had Kat laughing aloud. Briley looked like Kat handed her a winning lottery ticket.

Deborah took a sip of her orange juice before speaking. "That's generous of you, dear. I'm not sure what long term plans I'm going to make, but if you're sure, I would love to stay with you."

"Mom," Kat said. "I wouldn't have offered if I didn't mean it. I still have a few things that need to be renovated, but the guest room is good to go."

"I would really love that," Deborah said.

As soon as their orders arrived, the discussion turned to wedding plans.

"Have you decided on what you're going to wear?" Kat asked Briley and Leah while cutting into her pancakes.

Briley and Leah shared a look. "Leah has decided on a dress, but I'm not sure whether I want a dress or pants. Leah and the kids are visiting Madison next weekend and they're going dress shopping. I figured you and Mom could go with me. That is, if you don't have plans with Dylan, or she could come with us."

"Next weekend I have my second envelope date with Emma, but after lunch, I can join you for a couple of hours before I have to get ready for dinner with Dylan." She high-fived Briley over the table top.

"What colors have you decided on?" Deborah asked.

Leah answered since Briley's mouth was full of waffle. "Briley has given me control of the wedding, with only a few must haves from her. The colors are ivory and rose. I wanted classic over anything else. Our main flowers are lilies and roses. We're keeping it small, under a hundred people. We've already booked the Rosewood for the event."

Kat's eyes widened slightly, but she quickly masked her surprise. The Rosewood was one of the most sought-after venues for any big event in Garriety. Usually they were booked at least ten months in advance and didn't come cheap. On one hand, she was glad they were going all out for the ceremony and on the other, she wasn't sure she could spend so much money on a few hours.

"I figured since this was the last time I'm getting married, I should make it count." Leah held up her glass and Briley clinked it with hers.

"Darn straight. I didn't think we'd be able to get it booked, but Ashley helped me out. It cost me the promise of Danishes for the next few weekends. A price I'm willing to pay, besides the venue of course."

Kat smiled when Briley blushed after Leah kissed her on the cheek. "Well, I for one can't wait until you're married. I've loved seeing every minute of the beginning of your happy ever after."

"And we've loved having you tag along," Briley said.

"And for the record," Leah said, with a cheeky grin, "we're also enjoying your fairy tale story."

"Yes, well, I am too." It was nice spending time with them. She hadn't realized how much she'd missed it until now. She loved spending time with Dylan and Emma, but she needed to make more of an effort to juggle everyone else in her life. Since her mom was moving in with her, it would make it easier for them to spend some time together every day.

"So," Kat said, once they were in the restaurant's parking lot, "I guess I'll see you losers on Monday." She swung Griffin into her arms and danced her around. She would miss them when they went on their planned fishing trip, but knew they would have fun. She deposited a squealing Griffin into Leah's arms, kissed her on the forehead, then drew Leah into a hug. "Be safe."

"We will," Leah said.

"And you." Kat engulfed Briley in a bear hug. "Listen to everything everyone else says. Not like last camping trip."

Briley returned the hug just as enthusiastically. "Geez, you set one tent on fire."

Kat waved when their car drove away with a promise from her mom that she would help her get her stuff moved over after work, then they were having dinner with Dylan tonight. If someone would have told her two years ago that this would be her life now, she would laugh at them. Thank God her previous dreams weren't aligned with her current reality. She would have missed so much.

She turned up "Heaven Is A Place on Earth" on the radio and sung along all the way to work.

Chapter Twenty-six

Dylan shook her hands out and bounced on the balls of her feet. Her nerves had been getting the better of her all day. Tonight, she was having dinner with Kat and her mom. Emma was going to be spending the evening with Iris, putting together her new Lego set.

This felt different than meeting Ian's parents. Kat had already explained about the relationship with her mom, or lack of one, but insisted her mom was trying. That didn't calm Dylan's nerves any, but for Kat's sake, she would reserve judgment until she met Kat's mom.

She smoothed the green sweater she had pulled on after her shower and looked in the mirror. Kat had said casual, but she hadn't said what kind of casual. Casual at home was sweatpants, but there was no way she was meeting Kat's mom in sweatpants. She'd settled on the sweater and a pair of black slacks. She'd had them tailored last year, and had breathed a sigh of relief when they fit properly. There was no way she could afford another pair right now. There was simply no budget for it.

Her hair was down, per Kat's request, and she was happy to oblige her in this one thing since Kat never asked for much. She slipped her feet into a pair of black high heels and turned the bedroom light out before making her way into the kitchen where Iris and Emma were making dinner.

"Mom, you look really pretty."

"Thanks, sweetie."

"Emma's right. You look nice," Iris said.

"You'll be fine, Mom. Kat's there and she won't let anything bad happen to you."

"No, she won't." With lots of kisses all around, Dylan left and drove to Kat's house. At lunch, Kat had also informed her that her mom was temporally moving in with her.

All the downstairs lights were on and one upstairs when Dylan pulled into Kat's drive. She killed the engine and stared at the door until it opened, and an impossibly sexy Kat was leaning against the door frame. By looking at Kat, she guessed their casual wear was the same, considering Kat was dressed in a pair of blue slacks and a gray sweater.

When Dylan was a foot away, Kat pulled her into her arms, and kissed the top of her head. Being in Kat's arms was one of the most wonderful feelings she'd ever had and it didn't hurt that Kat always smelled amazing. She kept her arms wrapped around Kat but moved her head enough to place a kiss on Kat's neck. The tightening of Kat's arms around her would have spurred her on if they were alone.

Dylan pulled back and placed a tender kiss on Kat's lips. "You look dashing." Kat's answering grin set Dylan's heart racing. What this woman did to her.

"Let's just say you bring out the dashing in me, Ms. Lake." Kat stepped back and twirled Dylan before bringing them flush. "You always take my breath away."

If she wasn't already falling in love with Kat, she would be now. She smiled and smoothed the side of Kat's hair where it had recently been shaved, feeling a jolt of pleasure when Kat shivered. Her grin faded when Kat kissed her. Before the kiss could progress into the danger zone, Dylan pulled back and rested her hands on both sides of Kat's face.

"Didn't you tell me earlier I was having dinner with you and your mom this evening?"

"I did. Yes." Kat moved to allow Dylan to go ahead of her. When they both stepped into the living room, they stopped short when they spotted Deborah sitting on the couch sipping from a tea cup with Stripes lounging beside her. "Mom."

Jesus, they'd been caught making out like teenagers.

Deborah stood and placed her cup on the coffee table and stepped up to them. Stripes bounded off the back of the couch and raced upstairs. He was smart enough to know when to get out of Dodge. Kat placed her hand at the small of Dylan's back and nudged her forward.

"Mom, this is my girlfriend, Dylan. Dylan, this is my mom, Deborah."

Kat seemed so unsure, Dylan slipped her arm around Kat's waist and held out her other hand to Deborah. "It's nice to meet you, ma'am." While Kat and Briley had similar features, it was apparent that Kat took after her mom. The same smile and nose. Deborah was a beautiful woman and Dylan was getting a taste of what Kat would look like in later years.

Deborah sandwiched Dylan's hand between both of hers. "It's so nice to meet you. Even though I've been out of my daughters' lives, I've kept up with them. And may I say, I've been waiting for you a long time. I've never seen Katherine so happy."

Kat moved forward and swept her mom into a

hug. "Thank you."

"Don't be silly, Katherine. You'll always be my baby and I want you to be happy. That's all I've ever wanted for you girls. Now," she pushed Kat back to Dylan's side, "dinner's ready."

Dylan kissed a shell-shocked Kat on the cheek, then followed Deborah into the kitchen. In times like these, Dylan knew Kat would need a few moments to get herself together.

Deborah placed her hand on Dylan's arm. "I'm looking forward to getting to know you, and Leah as well. Maybe all three of us could find the time to have dinner together."

"I think that would be lovely. If you wanted, I could invite my mother as well."

"I would." Deborah fondled the pearls around her neck. "In the future, if it's all right with you, I would also love to meet your daughter."

Dylan had seen deadbeat parents before but that wasn't what she was seeing in front of her. Deborah had acknowledged to both Kat and Briley that she'd made mistakes and was owning up to them. Dylan wouldn't hold anything against her, not for the path that grief had sent her off to. If it hadn't been for her mom, she wasn't sure where she would be now after Ian's death. "She'll be at the cookout tomorrow. You can meet her then."

"That's lovely," Deborah said.

"And you'll get to see her again at Halloween."

"I can't wait." Deborah shook her head. "Briley's already asked if Leah needed to make me a costume as well."

"Wait. What?" Kat chimed in, standing in the doorway to the kitchen. "What outfit did you pick out?"

Kat said it so casually, Dylan wouldn't have thought anything about it, but she knew better. Kat had tried and failed to find out what Briley and her family was wearing for Halloween. Dylan was starting to get the feeling this was a bigger deal then she'd first thought. Maybe she shouldn't have waved it off when Kat had asked if they wanted to dress up.

"Not telling," Deborah said, waving her finger in the air. "Briley has already informed me that you are not to know. She's looking to win another spot in the paper."

"Paper?" Dylan asked when they all sat down at the table.

Kat set the platters of baked lemon chicken, a rice dish, and steamed vegetables on the table. "There is a costume contest every year. Last year they won as a family for the Incredibles. First place wins five hundred dollars. They gave Evan and Griffin their winnings for Christmas spending money."

Dylan toyed with her fork. "Baseball outfits won't get us a win, will they?" She already knew the answer before she'd even asked.

"Nope." Kat reached across the table and picked up Dylan's hand. "But, that's okay. This year I want you to be comfortable with us. But, next year, all deals are off."

"Promise?"

"Promise."

Conversation flowed easily over dinner. After dinner, Dylan joined Deborah in the living room while Kat cleaned up in the kitchen.

"So, tell me a little about yourself, Dylan."

Dylan smiled and ran through the basics of her

life. She didn't gloss over Ian's death and they were both quiet after she finished.

"I'm sorry, dear. I know how hard it is to say goodbye to someone you love."

"It's never easy, but when it's with someone you pledged your life to, it shakes you to the core. I loved Ian. Very much, but…"

"But." Deborah encouraged her to go on.

"At the beginning, I felt like I was betraying what we had by being with Kat. No, not by being with her, but feeling more for her then I did for him."

"I don't think that's the case at all," Deborah said. "I think that your love is just different. We love each of our partners differently, but that love doesn't diminish what we felt for the previous ones. They are different people; of course you're not going to love them the same. Katherine's needs are going to be different than Ian's. There is no reason why you would approach your feelings for Katherine the same way you would for Ian."

"I never thought about it that way before. Honestly, I'm not sure Ian and I would even be together now."

"Stop."

Startled, Dylan looked up, but relaxed when Deborah scooted close. "Why worry yourself over matters that, in the long run, don't matter? You'll never know what you would have done. Don't dwell on the past." Deborah closed her eyes. She opened them, and tears glistened. "You can't live in the past. Hold onto those memories but don't let them pull you down. You've got something good with Katherine. I just met you and it's clear to me."

Dylan surged forward and pulled Deborah into a

hug. That was exactly what she needed to hear, and it seemed exactly what Deborah needed to say. That's how Kat found them a few minutes later. Dylan accepted the Kleenex Deborah handed her and they both wiped their eyes and nose.

"Everything okay?" Kat looked from Dylan to Deborah, worry evident on her face.

"It's wonderful, dear," Deborah said.

"I'm fine," Dylan said.

"Well, if you're both sure." Kat handed Dylan and Deborah each a small bowl filled with what looked like vanilla ice cream and cookie and brownie pieces. "It's not the fanciest dessert, but it's delicious."

They finished their dessert and not long after that, Deborah excused herself to go to bed. Once they were alone, Kat sat on the couch and pulled Dylan into her arms.

It didn't take long for Kat to say something. "You sure you're okay?"

Dylan straightened and placed her hand in the center of Kat's chest. Kat was gorgeous, that was a fact, but it was more than that. She genuinely cared, and Dylan didn't know how she'd gotten so lucky. "Your mom reminded me not to live in the past. Time can't be undone, and all we can do is move forward. I'm ready for that." Dylan waited, and it didn't take long for a smile to grace Kat's enticing kissable lips.

"I'm ready for whatever you are."

"I know, but I've still been holding back, and I don't want to anymore. I..." Dylan blurted out what weighed on her mind for weeks. "I love you, Kat."

Kat closed her eyes and tightened her hold on Dylan.

"Please don't cry." Dylan scooted up and pushed

Kat back to recline on the couch, then lay fully atop Kat and rested their foreheads together. Kat cupped Dylan's chin and gave her a warm and loving look, laced with passion. Dylan had never seen so much emotion in anyone else's gaze that was directed at her.

"I love you too. So much." Kat captured her lips in a slow dance of power that had them both breathing heavy when they pulled apart.

"I love you, but I'm not ready for the next step…"

Kat placed a hand on Dylan's lips. "One step at a time. No pressure." She threw her head back and laughed. "You make me so happy. You have no idea. So happy."

"Believe me, I have an idea. I feel the same way about you. I don't want to hold back with you. I want to jump with you. All in."

"Without a net."

"Or a harness."

"Off the tallest building."

"The highest roller coaster." They both giggled, and Dylan relaxed into Kat's arms and rested her head on Kat's chest, listening to the beat of Kat's heart. "I love you, darling."

"Oh, Dylan. I think I've loved you since the moment I laid eyes on you."

Chapter Twenty-seven

Kat retired to bed with a smile and woke up with one and a pep in her step. Dylan loved her…and called her 'darling', the endearment turning her smile into a grin. She was never one for calling past girlfriends endearments. However, what she felt for Dylan far surpassed her feelings for any past girlfriends. She'd have to come up with an endearment for Dylan. Honey? Baby? Dearest? None of them sounded right for what Dylan was to her. It had to be spontaneous and said in 'the moment' as she was sure 'darling' was for Dylan.

She hated to let Dylan go last night after they declared their love for each other, but it was already late, and Dylan had to help her cousin get ready for the cookout today. Something Kat wasn't as scared about today as she was yesterday. There was a buzz running through her that she'd never felt before and she prayed to whoever was listening that it would never leave.

At the bottom of the stairs, she inhaled and groaned when coffee wafted her way.

"Good morning, Mom." Kat helped herself to some coffee before turning back to the table.

"It seems like it for you."

Kat felt her cheeks heat from a blush. "It is. Dylan told me she loved me last night for the first time."

"Come sit." Deborah patted the chair next to her. "Did you say it back?"

"Yes." Kat held the coffee cup between her hands. "I love her, Mom, and it feels really good. I was scared if I told her before she told me that I would end up scaring her off. We've known each other for close to seven months, but we've only recently started dating." She wasn't sure why she was opening up to her mom, but it did feel good, but there was still a part of her that was waiting for her mom to take up and leave. She knew only time would heal those wounds.

"Dear, when I saw you on Briley's porch, I could tell. I'm so glad you and Briley are happy. I really am. I want to make things right between us." She took a sip of her coffee. "It was hard after your father died."

"You don't have to—"

"No, I need to say this. Briley and I have already talked, but you and I haven't." She pressed her fingers on her mouth for a moment, then took a breath. "I shouldn't have taken out my grief on you and your sister. It was wrong, but it felt like something inside of me died, when he did. We always knew, barring anything unfortunate, he would die before me and we were both prepared for that, but I never dreamed it would be a motorcycle accident."

"He was so happy to get that motorcycle."

"I blamed myself for a long time because I was the one that bought it for him. I know it wasn't my fault, but it still felt like it. Like I was the one that set it in motion." A sad smile appeared. "He swept me off my feet and I only gave the age difference pause for a moment, then thought, to hell with it, this is the man I want to spend my life with."

"He was amazing."

"You have no idea. The first few years of our marriage was like a dream, then you and your sister came along, and everything seemed to click. We had our problems like any long-term couple does, but never for a moment did I ever think of leaving him."

Kat furrowed her brow. "What kind of problems?"

"Normal problems. Money, time, work. We were always faithful to each other. He would have rather died then to hurt any of us in that way. I pulled away from you both and I felt like I was doing the right thing after he died. I didn't want to be the cause of the same thing happening to you that happened to him. I lied when I said it was because you both looked and acted like him. How could I fault you two for loving him as much as I did? But I see now that it was a mistake. You two didn't really have anyone to turn to when he died." She stood and took what looked like a breakfast casserole out of the oven and placed it on the table.

"I'm not going to lie. It hurt when you secluded yourself away from us. At first, I thought it was from grief, but it seemed to grow worse over time."

"I've tried to keep in touch sporadically, but nothing like I should have. I should have been here with you both and I'm sorry that I wasn't. I've been too hard on you both. None of this was either one of your faults. Katherine, please forgive me for my short-sightedness. I do love you. So much."

Kat gulped back tears, stood, and engulfed her mom in a hug. "I love you too. I'll need time to realize you're really back, but I'm so glad you are. I didn't realize how much I missed you until I saw you standing on Briley's porch." She chuckled. "I was freaking out when Briley called me to tell me you were here."

"I don't want it to be like that."

"Neither do I."

They sat back down. Kat thanked her mom when

she served them both some casserole. "I always vowed I would never be the kind of mother to my kids that you were to me, but now that I'm an adult, I can sort of see your point. I don't want to dwell on the past, though. We still have things to work through and I wouldn't be opposed to group therapy if that would help."

"I think that's a good idea. I will fail, Katherine. That's a given, but I promise not to run."

"Then I promise not to avoid you."

Deborah held her cup up and Kat clinked hers against it.

Kat took a bite of the casserole. "This casserole is really good."

"It's your grandma's recipe. I'll write it down for you."

"I would like that."

"What time do we have to leave for the cookout?" Deborah asked.

Kat glanced at the kitchen clock that read a little after nine. "We can leave at eleven. That way I can meet Dylan's cousin before a lot of the other guests arrive."

"Nervous?"

"Not as much as I was. I know that Dylan and I have a way to go, but I like where it's going. I don't want to rush into anything. I don't want to mess this up."

"You're doing fine. Which brings me to another point. I wanted to apologize to you for giving you such a hard time about your accounting job. I shouldn't have."

"I shouldn't have gotten so upset with you because I knew you meant well, but this is something I had to do."

Deborah patted Kat's hand. "You're so like your

father in that respect. He did always go after what he wanted. Even if it was the hardest decision he'd ever made."

"Well, he went after you and got you, so I would say any other decision after that would be child's play. I think Briley inherited that from him. Leah was hesitant at first, but things worked out the way they were supposed to."

"They did."

As soon as they were finished eating, Kat shooed her mom away, so she could clear the table and put the leftovers away. Her mom's openness wasn't something she expected, but Kat would do her best not to hold her misdeeds against her. Group therapy would be for the best. She'd text Briley on Monday.

There was still a little time before she had to get ready, so she searched for and found Stripes in his cat tree, then harnessed him up for a quick walk. She found her mom in her room. Kat knocked on the door and opened it when Deborah called out. "We're going for a quick walk. Care to join us?"

"Give me a few minutes."

"Take your time; we'll be downstairs." Kat scooped Stripes up and headed to the living room. "Stripes, I do believe this is what they would say is a turning point in any story. Scary stuff buddy, but so, so worth it."

※※※※

Dylan got into a rhythm as she washed and peeled the last of the potatoes for the potato salad. "All done," she called out.

Macy grabbed the bowl and carefully placed

the potatoes in the pot of salt water on the stove then turned the burner on. "What time is Kat and her mom coming by?"

"She texted and said they were leaving the house at eleven." Dylan had felt light all morning and didn't even try to keep the smile off her face. Her mom knew something had changed when she woke up that morning. It was nice to not hold her feelings for Kat inside.

Macy picked up a pickle and bit into it, then cocked her head. "Did you get laid?"

Dylan grinned. "Nope."

"Something happened." Macy snapped her fingers. "Tell me." She ushered Dylan to the table.

She knew it was only a matter of time before Macy sensed something was up. "Last night, I told Kat that I loved her."

"Shut up. Tell me everything."

"I love her, Macy. I really do. It scares me, but isn't it supposed to?"

"All the good kind does."

"I told her I loved her, and she said she has loved me since she first saw me."

"That woman is smooth."

"You have no idea. She ticks every box that I didn't even know I had written down. It's hard to describe."

"You don't need to explain. I understand. Harold does that for me. When I first met him, I was like there is no way I'm dating a man named Harold. It sounded so old, but then I got over myself quick and snatched that man right up. I know Aunt Iris doesn't exactly like him, but he's always treated me as his equal. It was hard when we realized we couldn't have children, but you know what? We're enough for each other and we have Emma to spoil rotten." Macy nodded to the kitchen window where they could see Emma and Harold on the swing set. "Our life is full."

"I wasn't sure about him at first either. He was so cocky, but I quickly came to see what you saw in him and I hope you give Kat that same consideration."

"We're not going to tie her down and question her." Macy leered. "Or would you like that so you could have your way with her? Unless you've already had your way with her?" She waggled her eyebrows.

For a moment, Dylan hesitated. "I'm not ready for that step…yet."

"Mind if I ask why?"

"Sex complicates things."

"It also enhances them. You've known her for months. Is she really the type of woman to only focus on the sexual aspect of your relationship?"

"No, she's not." Dylan sighed and closed her eyes, but quickly opened them when Macy took her hand and squeezed it. "It's been a long time, Macy. What if I suck?"

Macy snorted. "Well, I'm sure she would like that."

"Oh, God," Dylan groaned, "you're bad."

They both laughed. "Seriously though, you love each other. It's okay to be scared, but don't let that hold you back. Talk to her about this. Communication is key. I know you had a successful relationship with Ian, but even I can tell this is different. If the way you and Emma talk about her is any indication, Kat would do just about anything for you two."

"She would. I know she would. I will talk about this with her tomorrow. I'll surprise her with lunch."

"She's working on a Sunday?"

"Her schedule is packed until mid-December. She and her two employees are taking a week off for Christmas." Dylan looked at her phone when it beeped, then looked up at Macy. "Kat's here."

"Don't keep her waiting. We'll talk more later."

After a quick glance in the foyer mirror, Dylan made her way to the front door and out of the house. Kat stood in the yard talking with Deborah and Iris. She proceeded down the steps and wrapped her arms around Kat, kissing her. "Hello."

"Hello," Kat said, her smile lighting up her face.

"It's good to see you again, Deborah," Dylan said.

"You as well, dear."

"Let's get inside," Iris said and ushered everyone in.

Macy was waiting in the living room for them and was cordial when introduced to Deborah and Kat. She waited until Deborah and Iris had walked out of the room to pounce on Kat. "So, Kat. What are your intentions toward my cousin?"

Dylan rolled her eyes, but kept her mouth shut. Kat could handle herself. She looked especially fetching today dressed in a pair of black Bermuda shorts and a blue V-neck t-shirt that showed off the muscles in her arms.

"I love your cousin and it's not my intention to deliberately hurt her."

Macy narrowed her eyes. "Did you rehearse that?"

Kat blinked. "Maybe, but it's the truth."

"Fair enough. I'm going to go check on everyone outside," Macy said, leaving them alone.

Kat flopped down on the couch beside Dylan. "How'd I do?"

Dylan was surprised that Macy had given in so easily. It frightened her to think about what Macy was up to. "You passed."

"Phew." Kat wiped her forehead with the back of her hand.

Dylan kissed Kat's jaw. "I love you."

"I love you."

"Everyone's supposed to be on their best behavior today," Dylan said, running her fingers underneath Kat's shirt and along her abs. God, she could touch her abs all day.

"Everyone but you." Kat stilled the hand.

"Sorry," Dylan said, not sorry in the least.

Kat stood, offering her hand to Dylan, who latched onto it, allowing herself to be pulled up and into Kat's waiting arms. "Don't be sorry. I don't mind you touching me. You can explore all you like, but maybe not in your cousin's living room with everyone waiting outside for us."

Dylan nipped Kat's neck before stepping away and pulling Kat along with her. "You're right. Now isn't the time, but soon."

"I can handle soon or later. We're in no hurry here."

"You're too good to me, Kat."

"Don't be silly. You're more than worth it."

"I hope you feel that way after meeting the rest of the family." Dylan paused. "They're good people but can come off as a little brash sometimes."

"You don't have anything to worry about. I'm glad to be here. Meeting your family is just one step in the process and I'm excited to check them all off."

Dylan nodded then lead the way outside. One thing was for certain. It was going to be a long day.

Chapter Twenty-eight

"Reeva, can you go grab a couple of boxes of flooring, so we can see what it's going to look like?" It was early, but Kat had wanted to get a bunch of things checked off for this build. The clients for this particular build would be back in Garriety in three weeks to pick up their new tiny house. Kat had been surprised, but pleased, that the couple had traveled a few hours to commission a tiny house from her. It just showed her that she was on the right track with the business.

"Sure thing."

Kat sat back on her heels and eyed the small space. It was more basic than some of the other models they had built but still had all the amenities one would need. It felt good to be able to create a home for someone. No matter the cost.

Once Kat had some time off, she wanted to finish her basement. She'd decided to turn it into a workout/game room. Briley had already requested a pool table and Leah had asked for a dart board. Kat had also decided to put a foosball table and air hockey down, per Emma's request. She was hoping to find a bunch of things second-hand. Since Evan had given up part of the basement to allow a media room to be built, Kat wouldn't have to worry about that for her house.

"Here we go," Reeva said. They spent the next fifteen minutes laying some pieces down to see what pattern they wanted to use. "I like the straight lines."

"Me too." It took them almost four hours, but they had the entire floor down. "Wow. That's nice."

"Hey, boss," Kyle said, sticking his head inside. "You have a visitor."

From the smirk on his face, she knew it was Dylan. "Tell her I'll be out in a minute."

"I sent her to your office."

Meeting everyone at the cookout wasn't as scary as Kat thought it would be. For the most part, everyone was lovely. She'd fallen into bed that night with a smile, like the one she sported now. She and Dylan were so busy during the week that not much time was available for them to get together. Lunch from Dylan was exactly what she needed.

"Go to lunch, Reeva."

"Aye, aye."

Even though dirty from work, she slipped inside the office and smiled when seeing Dylan sitting in her desk chair with lunch spread out on the desk. Dylan cupped Kat's cheeks as Kat leaned across the desk and planted a soft kiss on Dylan's lips.

"This is a nice surprise," Kat said, sitting down across from Dylan.

"I missed you, and Haley told me to get over my moping and bring you lunch. So, I did."

"Well, then." Kat held up her drink. "To Haley."

"To Haley."

Lunch was relatively quiet, Kat enjoying being with Dylan. Once their meal was finished, they both settled on the couch

"Are you ready for tonight?" Dylan asked.

Tonight, Dylan and Emma were spending the night with her. They were having a movie night, and

Kat had suggested it would be easier for them to stay over. Emma had accepted for them both before Dylan could get a word out. Even though Kat had tried to get her mom to spend the evening with them, she had opted to stay at Briley's. It was amazing to see how far her mom had come in such a short amount of time. She was flourishing at being a grandma. At this rate, Griffin, Evan, and Emma, Madison, and her family would get whatever they wanted.

"I am. I've got all the movies sorted, plus the food and drinks. I borrowed a few board games from Briley in case you two wanted to play. I changed the sheets on my bed for you and Emma and I'll take the guest room." At the look Dylan was giving her, Kat hurried on. "No arguments. My room has a bigger bed and will be perfect for the two of you. Or, if Emma wants her own bed, she can have the guest room and I'll sleep on the couch."

"If Emma chooses to sleep in the guest room, we can share your room, but only if that's something you're comfortable with."

"I would love to, but only if it's what Emma wants."

"Spending the night in a new place, Emma may have nightmares."

Kat hugged Dylan closer. "I figured. I'll probably be scared out of my mind, but as long as you're there to walk me through it, I'll be fine." She kissed Dylan's cheek. "I love you both and want you to stay, but if you think you shouldn't or it's too much, I'll understand."

"No, it's all Emma has been talking about all week. She's got three bags packed. If I didn't know any better, I would think she's moving in with you."

Kat fondled a curl of Dylan's hair. "I wouldn't

mind if you both wanted to leave some things at my place. I've cleaned out a drawer in my room and part of my closet, just in case."

Dylan stood and proceeded to straddle Kat's lap. Kat gripped her hips. "Did you now?"

Kat chuckled and pulled Dylan closer. "You bet. I want you both to know how much you mean to me and Stripes. He's also looking forward to two new play buddies."

"I see." Dylan wound her arms around Kat's neck and slipped her hands in Kat's hair. "Kiss me."

The kiss left them both breathless. Kat was about to push Dylan down on the couch when there was a knock on her door. Dylan hurriedly pulled away, then stood and gave Kat her hand. "That's your cue."

"I'll be right there," Kat called to the door and hugged Dylan, lifting her off her feet until they were nose to nose.

"Wow, look how strong you are."

Kat waggled her eyebrows. "Only for you."

"I'll take it, but I really do need to be going."

"I know."

Dylan kissed her when Kat set her back on the ground. "We'll see you tonight." Dylan ran her hand down Kat's tank top, then gripped it in her fist and pulled them flush together. "You do look so good in these."

"I know how much you enjoy them." Kat made a muscle and groaned when Dylan ran her fingertips along her bicep. She shivered, and Dylan laughed.

"Do you need me to bring anything tonight?"

"Just your daughter."

"That I can do. Have a good day." She stopped at the door. "I love you."

"I love you too."

When she joined the others, Kyle grinned knowingly. "Locking the door now, boss?"

Kat balled up a rag and threw it at him. "Shut up."

Five hours later, Kat opened her front door to a smiling Emma, but a somber Dylan.

"Ladies, come in." Kat took the three bags off Dylan and set them by the couch, then pulled Dylan into a one arm hug. What could have happened between lunch and now? "Love, you okay?"

"Fine, but Emma's a little tired."

Emma rolled her eyes. "I'm fine, Mom. Kat, I'm fine," Emma tried to convince them.

"She had a nightmare during her nap but insisted that we still come tonight."

Kat kissed Dylan on the cheek then knelt in front of Emma, who sat on the couch.

"Hey," Kat said.

"Yeah."

"It's okay to be upset or afraid. I used to have nightmares too. That's okay. I promise. We don't have to play games or build with Legos. We can eat dinner, watch a movie, then go to bed."

"With you and Mom?" Emma wiped at her eyes and Kat felt so helpless.

Kat looked to Dylan who nodded. "Yes, with me and your mom. Briley and I used to have sleepovers all the time." Kat braced herself when Emma flew into her arms. With a pleading expression, Kat looked up at Dylan, who motioned for her to get up and sit beside her on the couch. They sat there for a while in silence.

Kat was content to hold Emma until her tears stopped. Dylan's tight hold on her hand helped to keep her grounded. She didn't want to mess this up. One look at Dylan's face told her she wasn't.

"Here, sweetie." Dylan held a Kleenex up to Emma's nose and told her to blow, then she took a clean one and wiped her eyes. "Feeling better?" Emma nodded against Kat's chest.

"Sometimes a good cry is just what you need," Kat said, and stilled her movements when Emma rose up and looked at her.

"You cry too?"

"I do." She pushed the hair out of Emma's eyes. "Do you feel better?" Emma nodded. "Good. That's all that matters. You can cuddle me anytime and cry whenever you need it."

"Thank you."

"Of course." She pulled Dylan closer when Emma snuggled back into her chest.

"Kat's right. Crying helps us. And you know you can talk about your nightmare with us if you want, but you don't have to."

"Not now."

"Okay," Dylan said.

Kat leaned back and closed her eyes. If this was the hard times Dylan was talking about, then Kat thought she could handle it. It this wasn't, she hoped that whatever was to come she'd know the right thing to do. There was no way she wanted to fail either one of them. She knew one thing for certain, seeing Emma cry was one of the worst things she'd ever experienced in her life and she would do what was necessary to make sure it didn't happen too much in the future.

Chapter Twenty-nine

Dylan stared at herself in the full-length mirror in Kat's bedroom and had to admit she looked good in her ball player outfit. She also knew if she looked good, Kat would look phenomenal. Halloween had crept up on them quicker than either one of them expected.

She and Emma had arrived at Kat's an hour ago to get ready. Iris would join them at six o'clock.

It had taken a bit of convincing on Kat's part to allow Emma to spend the night with Briley and Leah after the festivities. Briley had asked, and Emma had said yes, stating that they would be across the street if Emma needed Dylan.

Briley and her family were going to watch movies after trick or treating and Emma felt excited about it. Kat had convinced her that it would be a good thing and they were only a phone call and a few hundred feet away. Dylan had only given in when she'd sat down with Briley, notebook in hand, and walked her through the process of cleaning Emma's prosthetic and how to care for her. Briley became so engrossed in what she was saying, Dylan knew Emma was in good hands.

The thought both scared and excited her. For one, it would be her baby's first sleepover without her present and for another, it would be her and Kat's first sleepover alone. It would be a lie if she said she wasn't nervous, but over the last month, Dylan realized she was ready to take the next step. Their kisses were nice, but she wanted more. Kat's willingness to allow Dylan to set the pace for their relationship was admirable but for the first time in a long time, Dylan was excited and looking forward to what the night would bring. Even if all they ended up doing was sleeping, she knew being held in Kat's arms would be enough.

With one final look in the mirror, she headed downstairs to join the rest. Kat was standing by Emma, who was holding a baseball shirt clad Stripes. The sight of all three of them almost took her breath away. How had she gotten so lucky? As if she could feel Dylan thinking about her, Kat looked up.

Kat whistled. "You are the nicest looking shortstop I've ever seen."

Dylan rolled her eyes. "Just because I'm short doesn't mean I would be the shortstop." At the bottom of the stairs, she made a twirling motion with her finger and Kat turned around with her arms out stretched. "Nice."

"Only for you, love. Only for you."

Dylan turned to Emma, whom Kat had helped dress. "I think we make a good team."

"We're awesome, Mom."

"We are."

"Come on," Kat said, calling her over.

For the first time she noticed her mom. "Hey, Mom."

"Hello, dear. Join them so I can get a picture."

Kat knelt on one side of Emma's wheelchair while Dylan knelt on the other side. Emma still had her prosthetic on, but she had been tired all day and Dylan wanted her to have fun and not tire out so easily.

After the picture was taken, she stood and slipped

her arms around Kat's waist. "Are you ready for this?"

"Born ready."

"Kat's already promised to help me get the most candy. I'm in a wheelchair, I'm sure I'll get more."

"Emma." Dylan couldn't believe she'd said that.

"Mom, it's true. Don't worry, I'll share with everybody."

"That's…never mind." She kissed the top of Emma's head.

"Now, say bye to Stripes," Kat said. "He can't go with us."

Ten minutes later, they were standing in Briley and Leah's living room and Dylan had to pick her jaw up off the floor. Kat hadn't been lying when she said they went all out for Halloween. Their theme this year had been D.C. villains. Briley was the Joker. Leah was the Riddler. Evan was Two-Face and Griffin was Catwoman. When Kat had said Leah was making the costumes, now she believed it. They were well-made and fit each of them to a T. Briley looked so smug that Dylan vowed that she, Kat, and Emma would be competing for the family prize next year. She didn't see how anyone would beat them this year.

She leaned into Kat and whispered in her ear. "Next year that family prize is ours." The smile she got from Kat in return was well worth all the time it would take to make their costumes for next Halloween.

"So," Briley said, rubbing her hands together. "We get candy first then head downtown for the contest."

Evan added smugly, "We've got this."

Briley beamed and they high-fived each other.

"Now, let's not get too overconfident," Leah said. "The last thing we want to do is jinx ourselves."

"Be real, Tiny. We've got this and if we don't win then none of the judges are D.C. fans."

"Let's go," Leah said, then leaned down to speak to Emma. "Are you ready for tonight?"

"Yes. You guys may win the contest, but I'm going to get the most candy. You can't beat a kid in a wheelchair."

The room was dead silent until Briley spoke up. "Well, she's got us there."

"Briley."

"What, Kat? She does. I know Emma is a capable little girl and she's right. You'll share though, right?"

"You bet. We're in this together."

"Yes, we are." Briley fist bumped her.

Dylan decided not to intervene and to enjoy the moment for what it was…Emma bonding with them. She knew Emma would be in safe hands tonight and seeing them all joking together made that point clear. Now, she could calm down and do the one thing she'd been thinking about all morning. Getting Kat into bed.

The night dragged on longer than Dylan expected. Briley and her family won for family in the Halloween contest, plus Leah and Briley came in first and second place for individual costumes. Three hours later, she and Kat were headed back to her house.

Emma had said her goodbyes, then settled on the couch with Evan and Griffin to watch a movie. Leah had promised to look after her as if she was one of her own.

Now, her nerves started up. Kat let her hand go when they walked into the living room, so she could set the alarm system. Kat had told her their neighborhood was one of the safest in Garriety, but it never hurt to be safe.

Dylan melted into Kat's arms when she slid them around her waist from behind. "Long night?" Kat nuzzled the side of Dylan's neck.

"It was, but worth it. I know Emma enjoyed herself."

"I did too. I'm kind of sorry Briley won. She'll be holding that over us until next year."

"That's all right. We may not win next year, but we're sure as hell going to give them a run."

Kat turned her around and pulled them flush together. "Your competitiveness is such a turn on."

"Is it?" Dylan slipped her hands underneath Kat's shirt and ran her fingernails up and down her back. She felt satisfaction when Kat closed her eyes and moaned. "Do you want to know what turns me on?"

Kat's eyes popped open and widened. "Yes!"

"You, darling. You turn me on. Everything about you makes me hot. It takes all the self-control I have sometimes not to tear your clothes off."

"Oh, my love," Kat whimpered. "That's…" She wet her lips. "Yes. Yes." She nodded.

Dylan smiled at the endearment. It wasn't the first time Kat had used one, but she liked it when she did. Yet, she didn't think she'd ever seen Kat so out of sorts. "Am I coming on too strong?"

"Nope." Kat dipped her head and captured Dylan's lips in a quick kiss. "Not at all…but are you sure you want this?"

"I appreciate you asking, but yes, I'm sure this is what I want. I've been waiting for you for a long time. I want you and I plan on having you. Is this okay?"

"Dylan." She cupped her cheeks. "You can have me any way you want me."

"Really? Well." Dylan took a step back. "I would

love to see that uniform on the floor." Before Kat could take it off, she held a hand up. "But I need a shower first. Would you be opposed to taking a shower with me before we make love?"

Kat gasped, then grinned. "You know something. You surprise me every day. I would love to take a shower with you. Let me double check down here, then I'll join you upstairs."

"Okay." Dylan stepped back then turned and headed up the stairs toward Kat's bedroom. Instead of waiting for Kat, Dylan decided to get started without her. She turned the shower on, then stripped and climbed inside. If it was anyone else, she would be self-conscious about her body, but time after time Kat had made it clear that she desired her, and Dylan had decided not to doubt her.

Dylan leaned her forearms against the shower wall and let the water beat down on her back. She held her breath in anticipation when the shower door opened and Kat entered. When arms circled her waist, she let Kat pull her back against her.

"You started without me?" Kat accused, then turned Dylan's head and kissed her, Kat's tongue seeking entrance. Dylan turned, leaned against the wall, and pushed Kat away. The questioning look on Kat's face almost made her laugh. "What?"

"This is just a shower. My first time with you isn't going to be in the shower." Dylan let her eyes stray and sucked in a breath at how ripped Kat really was. She admired her firm breasts with the dark rosy nipples now hardened to points from the warm spray of water. Or was it from excitement and anticipation? She reached out and ran her fingers down between Kat's breasts, then caressed her abs.

"Then stop that," Kat hissed.

"Sorry." Dylan stood while Kat slowly looked her over. The apparent pleasure in Kat's eyes at what she saw made Dylan warm.

"Are you sure you want to do this?"

"Yes. Very sure." Dylan nipped Kat's chin.

Kat groaned. "Okay, let's hurry so we can go play."

Dylan laughed and slipped her arms around Kat's neck and stood on tiptoes to give her a sound kiss. The first touch of Kat's firm breasts against her was heavenly. "My darling, how I love you."

"I love you too. Tonight might be our first time, but I'm so invested in you I'm sure everything is going to be perfect."

"You're so smooth." Dylan pulled back and allowed Kat to wash her, reveling in the lingering strokes of the warm washcloth over her body. "Hmm, wash me, not feel me up, or we won't leave this shower until the water turns cold and our skin wrinkles."

Kat laughed, and finished the job. Then Dylan did the same to Kat, fighting the urge to toss the washcloth aside and use her hands. When they dried off and Dylan lay back on the bed with Kat hovering above her, she knew the right decision that day was saying yes to ice cream with her. Kat had changed her life and she wouldn't have it any other way.

"You look way to serious, love. I'm going to have to do something about that." Kat leaned down and kissed her.

Dylan melted immediately into the kiss, grasping onto Kat's hips, her insides quivering with excitement at the light caress of Kat's fingers along her sides. Dylan barely caught her breath before pulling Kat flush against her. The feel of Kat's warm breasts with their hardened tips against hers sent Dylan's mind into overdrive. Kat's touch sent chills along her spine.

"You're stunning," Kat managed to say between kisses.

Dylan squirmed when Kat kissed down her neck to a breast and closed her mouth around a taut nipple, sucking lightly and stroking it with her warm tongue.

"Yes, yes. Darling, right there." Dylan tried to pull Kat back down when she kissed her way back up to her mouth.

"I plan on taking my time with you. We have all night, love, and I plan on taking advantage of that."

"Less talk. More action." Dylan groaned. God, she really did love this woman. Her eyes closed as Kat trailed opened mouthed kisses down her body. Dylan lost herself in the sensations of Kat loving her.

Chapter Thirty

Kat slowly became aware of her surroundings and blinked her eyes open. Her arms tightened around the sleeping woman when she glanced at the clock on the nightstand and noticed it was only five-twenty-six. Falling back asleep was out of the question, but she still closed her eyes, enjoying the warmth of Dylan snuggled against her. She nuzzled against the back of Dylan's neck, breathing in her warm scent.

The previous night was an eye-opener as they learned each other's bodies. Dylan was so responsive, and Kat enjoyed finding that spot on her inner thigh that drove Dylan wild when gently bitten.

This feeling of completeness was new and instead of being afraid, she decided to keep diving. She was worth it. Dylan was worth it and most important, they were worth it. She moved the hair away from Dylan's neck and kissed right below her ear. When Dylan squirmed, Kat stopped.

"Really, darling," Dylan said in a drowsy tone, "I didn't take you for starting something you couldn't finish."

Kat chuckled and pulled Dylan tighter against her. "Oh, I can finish."

"You're incredible, but I'm not really one for morning after sex. My body needs time to wake up. I hope that's okay."

"Of course it's okay. Remember, I don't ever want

to do anything that's going to make you uncomfortable. So, no to morning after sex. How about morning after sex in the shower?"

"Now, that is something I can get behind." Dylan turned in Kat's arms and ruffled Kat's mussed hair. "You are beautiful." Kat shivered when Dylan's hand dipped low on her hip. "I still find it surreal that you want me."

"Want you? I more than want you." Kat kissed her neck then looked into her eyes. "You've turned my life upside down." She pushed the hair out of Dylan's eyes. "In the span of a year and a half I started a new business and fell in love. That is fucking surreal. I get it. I can't believe you want me."

"I want all of you."

Kat pulled Dylan into her arms. Dylan pushed her away when Kat licked her shoulder. The sheet slid down, leaving Dylan's glorious full breasts with their puckered pink nipples on view. Kat bit her lip and moaned when remembering their weight and soft feel in her hands. She started to crawl to Dylan who laughed and scooted back from her. Kat was set to make her move when her phone chimed with Briley's ringtone. With a groan, she turned to Dylan. "It's Briley; this had better be important." She snatched the phone off the nightstand and put it against her ear. "Hello."

"Hey, Kat."

Briley sounded way too chipper for there to be anything amiss. "Wait a minute." She muted the call. "She's too chipper for anything to be wrong."

"I'm going to start the shower." Dylan slid off the bed, and Kat flopped onto her stomach, watching her walk away with an enticing sway to her hips. Dylan stopped at the bathroom door. "Join me when you're done."

"Damn." She unmuted the phone. "This better be important."

"Well. Not really. I was calling to see if you wanted to run."

"Are you serious?" Kat growled into the phone.

"Yes," Briley said, a bit hesitant. Then, "Uh. Did I interrupt something?"

"Yes, yes you did," Kat hissed into the phone. "You have shit timing, Briley. I've got to go."

"Well, how about breakfast? All of us. Emma did good last night. No nightmares."

"Good. Good." Kat jumped off the bed. "I'll see you later." There was no way she was going to miss showering with Dylan. "Bye." She threw the phone on the bed and high-tailed it to the shower. Yes, this was going to be a good morning.

An hour later, Kat turned from the coffee maker when Dylan wrapped her arms around her waist and pulled her into a kiss. "Good morning, love."

"It is a good morning," Dylan said, running her fingers underneath Kat's t-shirt. "An excellent one, in fact." She traced her fingers along the elastic of Kat's sweatpants.

"As much as I would love to," Kat pulled Dylan impossibly closer, "We're due at Briley's in ten minutes."

"I know; this bubble we've found ourselves in is nice."

"I know exactly what you're feeling." Kat didn't want this to end either, but they had lives and she was sure Emma would be wondering where Dylan was. She glanced at Dylan's neck where she'd expertly covered up the mark of their passion…one of the more visible marks. "I'm sorry about your neck."

Dylan narrowed her eyes. "I'm sure you're not. The smug look on your face after you noticed it is all the proof I need."

"I mean. I'm not sorry about the process and I'm sure you're not either, but I am sorry—" Kat paused and tried to mask the smile but failed. "Who am I kidding, I'm not sorry but I will be more careful in the future. I promise. I realize we're both adults and we have to be adults out in the world, but you make we want to be a kid again."

Dylan laughed and backed out of Kat's arms. "A kid, huh? So, you like to play?"

"You better believe it." Dylan ran into the living room, Kat quickly catching up with her, and they fell on the couch trying to catch their breath. "I love you."

"Darling." Dylan wrapped her arms around her neck. "I love you too."

Kat was enjoying being wrapped up in Dylan when her phone vibrated. "That would be Briley." She answered the phone, "On our way," then ended the call. "You ready, love?"

"Let's go. I loved our time together, but I am a bit anxious about seeing Emma."

Kat jumped up and held out her hand for Dylan. "Let's go. I already fed Stripes, so let's go feed ourselves." The walk across the street didn't take enough time in Kat's opinion.

Dylan pulled her to a stop before Kat opened the kitchen door.

"You okay?"

"Yes." Dylan closed her eyes and nodded. "I needed a moment."

"Take your time." Kat hugged Dylan until Dylan

pulled back. "Ready?"

"Yes."

Kat opened the back door for Dylan to enter. Conversation didn't stop when they walked in, but Briley smirked in her direction before Leah smacked her with the dish towel and mouthed 'behave'.

Emma was seated at the table, drinking a glass of orange juice. "Mom, I had a lot of fun."

Dylan kissed her daughter on top her head. "I'm so glad. Tell me about it."

Kat accepted the two cups of coffee Leah handed her, then sat across from Emma and Dylan.

"Breakfast will be ready in a few minutes. Briley, go wake our kids up."

Kat held back her own snicker when Briley did as she was told.

"Do you need some help, Leah?" Dylan asked, starting to stand, but Leah waved her off.

"Kat can help."

Kat jumped up and kissed the top of Emma's head before joining Leah at the stove.

"Love looks good on you, Kat," Leah said quietly.

"It feels good too." Kat pulled Leah into her side. "I hope you and Briley feel only a little of what I feel for Dylan."

"You've got it bad."

"You have no idea." She accepted the whisk Leah handed her, then started whisking the gravy on the stove. "Decided on an old-fashioned breakfast?" She snatched a piece of bacon from a platter and popped it in her mouth.

"Scoot over." Leah opened the stove and took out the biscuits. "It was Briley's choice this morning."

"Hey, Mom." Evan entered the kitchen, kissed

Leah on the cheek, then did the same to Kat. He paused, shook his head, got two glasses down from the cabinet, then continued to the fridge and poured orange juice for himself and Griffin.

Kat held back her laugh because he was still half asleep. She stood back while Briley wrangled a squirming Griffin into her seat. A moment later, Deborah walked into the kitchen. She looked more put together than all of them combined. That was saying something since Leah always looked more poised than anyone.

After all were seated at the table, Briley picked up her glass of milk and held it high. "To family."

"To family," everyone echoed.

An hour later, all the kids were situated in the movie room and the adults were seated around in the living room.

Kat jerked her head up when a wadded-up piece of paper hit her in the face. "Really, Briley?"

"You need to pay attention." Even as Briley said the words, she balled up another piece of paper.

"Don't." Kat shifted her attention from Dylan, who was seated on the couch with Leah and Deborah, to Briley. "Did you want something?"

"Dylan mentioned that you and Emma were going to be working on the camper Saturday and I was wondering if Griffin and I could join you?"

Kat turned to Dylan who nodded. "I suppose." She sighed. "If you must."

"Well, I don't want it to be a hardship."

Kat made a face and stuck out her tongue. "Shut up, dork."

"Then that gives me an idea," Deborah said. "While you girls are out with the kids, Leah and Dylan, why don't we all go out to lunch and get to know each other better? Dylan, you can invite your mom."

"That sounds wonderful, Deborah," Leah said, then stood when her phone rang.

When Leah stepped out of the room, Briley spoke up. "That's Madison."

Kat arched her brow. "Do you know all of her ringtones?"

"Of course. Why? It's not weird."

"I didn't say it was."

"You're face says it all, Kat."

"I would love to join you," Dylan said. "and I'm sure my mom will too."

Deborah patted Dylan's hand. "That's great."

Kat looked to Dylan, but she was still as relaxed as she was that morning. Good; she loved that Dylan got along with her family.

"You all should go to Barney's." Briley clapped her hands. "It's Spanish infused and awesome. They only serve six dishes, but you won't be disappointed. I'll make the reservation." Briley picked up her phone and was typing on it when Leah walked back in.

Leah took Briley's phone out of her hand and plopped down in her lap. "Madison wanted us to be the first to know." She smoothed the hair out of Briley's eyes.

"Know what, Tiny?" Briley relaxed in the recliner and tilted her head back to give Leah her full attention.

Kat took the opportunity to get up to sit beside Dylan, and took her hand, caressing the knuckles.

"Know that she's pregnant." Leah beamed.

Kat held back her snicker when she saw the blank look on Briley's face.

"That's great," Briley finally got out.

"You're not happy?" Kat asked.

"It's not that."

Leah chuckled. "Briley and I talked about this after she proposed. She's not sure how to feel about being a grandmother at her age."

Kat threw back her head and laughed. "Shit! Briley, you should be happy."

"I am. I am. I love them to death, but it's taken me more time to get used to the idea of being a grandmother. That's all. Of course, I'm happy. They're happy?" She asked Leah.

"Ecstatic."

"And you?"

"I'm also happy, but like Briley, it's taken some getting used to knowing I have a daughter and a granddaughter and grandson around the same age."

Everyone was silent until a little voice piped up from beside the couch.

"Shit."

Kat whipped her head around and her eyes latched onto Griffin, who a few minutes ago was down in the movie room.

"Really, Kat." Leah motioned for Griffin to come to her. "We don't say those words."

"Why?"

"Because they're not nice."

"Why?"

Kat admired Leah's patience while Griffin kept asking why questions. Evan had just entered the room to hear the 'whys' and snorted, then scooped Griffin up and headed to the movie room. Leah's attention then fixed on Kat. "What?" Kat kept her gaze neutral, but inside she knew she was in trouble.

"Briley has to clean out the garage tomorrow.

She could use some help," was all Leah said.

"Fine." She glanced at Briley. "You can wipe that smirk off your face."

"You can wipe the ugly off your face." Briley mouthed, "Shithead," then threw the paper wad.

Kat caught the wad then lobbed it back across the room and smacked Briley in the face. "Don't mess with me. You'll lose, loser."

"Now, Kat," Dylan said, "shouldn't you two be setting a good example for the children?"

"I suppose." She squeezed Dylan's hand and didn't have time to react when another wad hit Dylan in the side of the face. Kat held in her laugh.

"On second thought. Kick her butt."

Kat snickered, then the warmth and love in Dylan's eyes snared her. She lost herself in their depths. This amazing woman wanted her. It all felt like a dream. A dream she didn't want to ever wake up from.

"Kat," Dylan said softly, and cupped her chin. "I love you."

"I love you too."

She pecked Dylan on the lips, then stood abruptly and turned to Briley. Briley audibly gulped and clung to Leah for protection. When Leah pried Briley's hands from around her, Briley scrambled up and over the back of the chair. Kat gave her a few seconds head start, then took chase.

Chapter Thirty-one

Today was another turning point in her relationship with the Lake women. Kat was both excited and terrified to be spending the afternoon alone with Emma. Thankfully, when Dylan had agreed to today, Kat hadn't seen any hesitation that she didn't want it to happen. She would never allow Dylan's trust in her to be diminished and would make sure nothing happened to Emma. They'd both decided today would be a good day to pick out things for the camper, which was a slow-going process.

She, Kyle, Reeva, Brandon, and Briley had fixed the exterior of the camper during a few late nights the previous month. With the five of them working, it had gone quickly. They'd put in new doors and windows, a new set of steps, and painted the exterior teal and grey per Dylan and Emma's instructions. It looked brand new from the outside. The interior was another story. It had been gutted, rewired, and new plumbing installed. Now the time had come to customize the camper to Dylan and Emma's needs.

Dylan had already given the okay for Emma to pick out any flooring she wanted for the living area and the bathroom, along with the light fixtures. Kat had to reassure her countless times that all the materials Emma would pick from would be left over from various jobs. What she hadn't told Dylan was that the stove and refrigerator weren't salvageable, and Kat had bought them new ones. If Dylan made a fuss, Kat was going to chalk it up to an early Christmas present. Since Kyle had become friends with the seller, they'd gotten a good price on both pieces. There was no way Kat was going to cut any corners when it came to her girls' lives.

The night before on the phone, Dylan had told her how excited Emma was about the planned day. Dylan quickly went over everything that needed to be done for Emma to have a fun day out. Kat would make sure Emma was always safe. It would make it easier since Briley and Griffin would also be joining them. Briley was working on a cedar chest at Kat's warehouse for a Christmas present to Leah, and was almost finished with it. It relieved a little bit of Kat's nerves knowing Briley would be there to help her, if needed.

She felt a bit better that Dylan wouldn't be alone today and, instead, was having lunch with her mom, Leah, and Deborah. Kat didn't foresee any issues arising from the lunch, since everyone seemed to get along. She knew Iris would fit right in.

Briley and Griffin would be joining them at the warehouse, so Kat headed out to pick up Emma.

When she pulled into the drive, the front door opened, and Emma walked out, followed by Dylan and Iris. Kat hopped out and approached them, readily accepting the hug Emma gave her, then she drew Dylan into her arms. "You look beautiful."

"Thank you." Dylan slipped her hand behind Kat's neck and brought her down for a kiss. "You look good enough to eat," she whispered, then slipped her hands underneath Kat's shirt and ran her fingernails down her back.

Kat cast a furtive glance at Iris and Emma, seeing

that Iris was straightening the collar of Emma's shirt, the two paying them no mind. "Now who's starting something they can't finish," Kat whispered back, but enjoyed the attention.

"You're mine tonight." Dylan kissed her lightly then pulled away. "Emma's really excited."

"Me too. I'll take good care of her."

"I know."

"Good. Good." Kat took her ballcap off and slicked a hand over her hair. "If you want, we can swing by before dinner and you can check out our progress."

"I would like that. Now go."

Kat held her hands up. "I'm going." She turned to walk away then pivoted back and kissed Dylan on the cheek. "You have a good day too."

"I will. Now go."

"Iris, you have a good day as well."

"I will, dear."

Emma was waiting by the truck and Kat hurried to her. "Ready for today?"

"I can't wait."

"Good." Kat opened the truck door. "It's a little high. Would it be okay if I lifted you up?"

"I trust you."

The warm fuzzy feeling she'd had since pulling into the driveway engulfed her. "Good, because I would never let anything bad happen to you." Kat placed her hands on Emma's sides, lifted her into the truck, then shut the door, raced around to the driver's side, climbed in, and started the truck. "Are you hungry?"

"Not really."

"Cool." Kat rubbed her hands, then stilled when a small hand touched hers.

"Are you okay?" Emma asked. "It's just me."

"I know. It's our first time being alone. I'm a little nervous."

"You'll be fine. I have faith in you."

Kat almost laughed at how serious Emma was being. "Thanks."

Twenty minutes later, Kat pulled into her spot in front of the warehouse and killed the engine.

"We should have our own handshake," Emma said.

"That's a great idea. How do you want to start?" Kat pulled the key out, unbuckled her seatbelt, then turned to Emma.

"Let's bump fists, then you shake my right hand and I'll shake your left, then we can air kiss and maybe add to it in the future."

Kat grinned at the enthusiasm that flowed off Emma in waves. It made her feel good that Emma had taken the time to think about this.

"Let's hop out and try it." Kat climbed out then rounded the truck and helped Emma down. She waved at Briley, who had a firm grip on Griffin. "Ready?" Kat couldn't keep the smile off her face as they went through the motions. "That was awesome."

"So cool." Emma clapped her hands. "Let's try again."

After two more times, they had it down pat. Kat grabbed Emma's backpack and her bag before they joined Briley.

"Hi Briley, Griff."

"Hey, Emma, what were you two doing?" Briley asked.

Kat slipped her arm around Emma's shoulders and pulled her into her side. "It was our secret handshake."

Briley nodded. "It is a rite of passage." She knelt in front of Griffin. "Ready?" At Griff's nod, they started in on a series of motions that Kat couldn't follow.

Kat looked down at Emma, who smiled up at her. "I like ours."

"Me too."

"All right." Briley stood. "I already unloaded the supplies I brought and set them with the rest of your stuff."

"Let's get started."

Once inside, Briley and Griffin went in one direction and Kat and Emma in the other. The last time they'd worked on the camper, Kat had Kyle help her set all their flooring samples by it. From the looks of the piles, Briley had brought all her extras with her.

"Let's see what we got."

Emma's eyes were huge, her mouth open in surprise. "There's so many."

"There is, but it gives us lots of options." Kat took a piece from each pile and divided them by wood and stone. She was partial to the grey or the bamboo, but this was Emma's choice. "What do you think?"

Emma walked from one to the other, then gestured to a grey granite stone. "I like these for the bathroom."

"Me too." Kat set her choice aside. "Now the living slash kitchen area."

"I can pick whatever I want?"

Emma's hopeful look was almost Kat's undoing. "You bet."

"I like them all."

"I know it's hard to pick, but is there one you like more?" Kat knelt next to her.

"No." She shook her head. "I like them all. Can

we mix them?"

"Not all of them. Let's see." Kat took out the same brand flooring and set them side by side. Dark grey, walnut, cherry, and bamboo.

"No, switch those two." Emma indicated which two with her finger.

Kat did, then stood. They really looked good together. "All right. It looks great. You sure?"

Emma gave an enthusiastic nod. "Yep. I like them."

"All right." Kat picked up her choices then set them on a bench beside the camper.

"Are we putting the floor down?" Emma asked, walking up to her.

"Nope."

"What are we doing?"

"Well." Kat turned and leaned back against the bench, then smiled when Emma did the same. "First we're going to pick out the light fixtures, then we're going to paint the inside."

"Really?"

"Yep, and I know how much you like to paint so I left a spare space on the wall about this big." Kat held out her hands to mimic a fourteen-inch square, "So, you can paint anything you want on it." She lifted Emma's backpack. "I had your mom pack your paints."

Emma turned and wrapped her arms around Kat's waist. "Thank you. Thank you."

"You don't have to thank me." Kat got down on her knees and pulled Emma into a hug. "I love you and your mom. This camper is for you two, so you two need to be the ones that decorate it."

Emma cupped her cheeks. "You're going camping with us, aren't you?"

"Wild bears couldn't keep me away."

Emma giggled. "I love you."

Kat choked back her tears then pulled Emma into a hug. "I love you and you can come to me for anything. I'll always be here for you. I promise."

"Pinky promise?"

"Pinky promise." Kat held out her pinky and Emma hooked it with hers. "Ready to get this party started?"

"What happens after painting?"

"Pizza."

Emma pumped her fist and grinned. "Yes! With mushrooms?"

"With mushrooms." Kat stood and, for the first time, realized she had an audience. Briley gave her a thumbs up then went back to Griffin, who was climbing on Kyle's back. She hoped Dylan's day was going as well as hers.

※ ※ ※ ※

For the third time since they'd left home, Iris stilled Dylan's fingers tapping on the dashboard. "I don't know why you're so nervous."

"It's the first time I'll spend with them without Kat present." She was trying not to have a mini freak out but was failing. From the selfie Kat had sent of her and Emma, she knew they were having a good time.

It wasn't as hard as she thought it would be to let Emma go with Kat, but it still left her anxious. She knew it was the next step in their relationship, and she trusted Kat, but Emma was her baby.

"She's as safe with Kat as with either one of us, or Macy and Harold."

"Are you a psychic? Because you always know the right thing to say."

Iris barked out a short laugh. "I'm a mother, remember? They're fine and we will be too. Kat loves Emma and she's going to be a wonderful mother."

"She will."

Iris hummed. "Is having more children something you've talked with Kat about?"

"It's not something we've specifically talked about, but I have a feeling she will want more."

"And you? I know, at one point, you mentioned having more children, but you haven't said anything in a while."

Dylan looked out the window. "With Ian, I thought Emma was enough. I couldn't see myself having more with him, but with Kat—"

"You want more?"

"I would be happy with only Emma for the rest of my life, but I wouldn't be opposed to having more with Kat."

"Good. I'm glad you're finally starting to think long term with her." She sighed. "I do believe Kat may be your Harold."

Dylan turned from the window to look at her mom when she slowed down at the stoplight. "What?"

"I think she's your Harold. I may not have liked him at the beginning, but I see how he treats Macy. He worships the ground she walks on. His love for her is evident as is Kat's for you."

"Wow."

"Don't tell your cousin I said that."

"I won't." Dylan grew quiet as Iris pulled into the parking lot. "You didn't think Ian was my Harold?"

"Look at me." Iris stroked her cheek. "As much

as I liked, even loved Ian, and yes, he did treat you amazing, I never felt like he was the one for you. Do I believe he would have been faithful and treated you like a queen had he lived, yes, but I also think you would have been missing out on something life shattering. I'm glad you met, fell in love, and married him. You were happy together and those are wonderful memories, so don't take what I'm saying the wrong way. You light up whenever Kat is even mentioned. I can see by the look on your face if you're thinking about her. It's more than evident how much you love her." She shook her head. "I'm saying this all wrong."

"No." Dylan drew her into a hug. "You're not. I love you and I understand. Some people in our lives are leading us to where we're supposed to be. My love for Ian eventually led me here."

"Yes. Take your love for Ian and tie it in a neat box and set it aside. It's time to take hold of your future with Kat. You both want a future together; now it's time for you both to take it."

Dylan kissed her mom on the cheek then stepped out and waited for her mom while she gave the keys to the valet.

"Fancy place," Iris whispered.

"It is." Dylan slipped her arm through her mom's and led her in. They were quickly taken to their table, where Deborah and Leah were already seated.

"I'm so glad you both could make it," Deborah said after they were seated and had given their drink order.

"We were happy to come," Iris said and turned to Leah. "I'm Iris, Dylan's mom."

"Leah, Briley's fiancée. It's nice to meet you." She turned to Dylan. "I'm not sure about you but I've already received several photos from my troublemakers that were suspicious."

Dylan swirled the wine in her glass. "I have a feeling by the time they get home that I'm going to have two paint speckled troublemakers as well."

At that moment both of their cell phones went off, alerting them that a text message had come through. Dylan couldn't hold back her laugh when she looked at the photo. Kat and Briley knelt behind Griffin and Emma and they all had paint moustaches.

"See," Leah said. "Troublemakers."

Dylan passed the phone to her mom. "But, would we have it any other way?"

"Never." Leah held up her glass and Dylan tapped it. "To our girls."

"To our girls." It might not have been what she expected, but it's exactly what she wanted.

Chapter Thirty-two

Kat ran around her living room picking up and putting away all of Stripes' toys. It seemed that while she was with Emma today, Stripes had decided to pull out and even destroy some of his toys. It was at that moment, Kat knew, she hadn't been spending enough time with him lately. She would change that in the future. He was important to her. After a quick cuddle and extra diced beef, Kat had enough time to shower and dress.

A glance at the kitchen clock let her know that Dylan would be there any minute. It was date night and Kat couldn't wait to get Dylan into her arms. Loving her was one of the easiest things Kat had ever done.

"I know, Stripes. I promise tomorrow you will get ample cuddles plus I'll even walk you around the block and stop by Mrs. Hanlin's house. I know how much you like her." Kat believed the only reason he enjoyed her neighbor's house so much was because Mrs. Hanlin kept a bag of ferret treats on hand and would give him a few pieces.

When the doorbell rang, she stopped at the foyer mirror and, satisfied with what she saw, pulled open the door and all her thoughts fled from mind. "Wow."

"I'm glad you like it." Dylan ran her hand down Kat's chest.

"Sorry." Kat shook her head. *Stop being a creep.* "You look amazing." And she did in a fitted skirt and damn near sheer top.

"You can look. That's why I wore it." Dylan sat on the couch.

Kat was still in awe of Dylan even after she shut the door. Dylan patted the spot beside her on the couch. Kat hurried over, greeted Stripes, who perched on a couch arm and turned his back, jumped down, then ran upstairs.

"Now that he's gone, come here," Dylan said. Kat readily sat beside Dylan.

"He's being pissy." Kat let herself be pulled into the warmth of Dylan's lips that had her melting. Time seemed to stand still for a moment, and she poured every ounce of love for Dylan into the kiss. She slid her hands along Dylan's thighs and squeezed when Dylan pulled back. Kat kept her eyes closed and enjoyed the way Dylan ran her fingers along her neck. Her eyes popped open when Dylan kissed the tip of her nose.

When Kat moved forward to capture her lips once more, Dylan placed her hand on Kat's chest.

"There's something I wanted to talk with you about. It's what I wanted to start with, but you always look delicious."

Kat kissed the palm of Dylan's hand, then sandwiched it between hers. "What's on your mind?" From the relaxed state Dylan was in, Kat knew it wasn't anything bad. At least she hoped it wasn't. Sometimes, Dylan had a really good poker face.

"Okay." Dylan nodded. "I know this isn't anything we've ever talked about, but I see us continuing to move forward and I think it's important to talk about it now before things get any more serious."

"Hey, I'm right here. Go on." Now she was starting to get a little worried, but would do what was necessary to make sure Dylan stayed relaxed. If what Dylan wanted to talk about was so serious that it could derail their relationship, Kat had to be one hundred percent focused on this moment. In her mind, there wasn't anything that would do that, but she would keep an open mind for both of their sakes and the sake of their future.

"I know you love me and Emma, but what if I told you I wasn't sure I wanted any more children? I'm not saying I don't, but we've never talked about more children and I think we need to."

"Children?" Dylan was talking about more children. That she hadn't expected, but Dylan was right; it was something they needed to talk about. Children meant a lifelong commitment and, unlike in previous relationships, this time the topic didn't leave her scared; it made her excited. Dylan wanted a future with her. She'd always known she wanted children and the slight fear she saw in Dylan's eyes would never do.

"Yes, children."

"Okay." Kat pecked Dylan on the lips. "I love you and Emma, and yes, I've always wanted a big family. I would love to have children with you, but it wasn't until I met you and Emma that I realized I didn't need anything else in my life to make me happy. If Emma's all we have, I would die happy."

Dylan's eyes widened slightly. "You do realize we're talking long term here, yes?"

"I know and it's making me happy and excited for the future. I didn't know I needed you until I met you and know I can't imagine my life without you in it."

"So, yes to maybe more children, but—"

"But I'll be satisfied with Emma."

"You're sure? I need you to be sure." Dylan wrapped her arms around Kat's neck.

"I'm sure. I'm not making light of this. Would I like more children, yes, I would, but would I be disappointed if we didn't have any more, no I wouldn't." She frowned. "I hope that makes sense. Either way would be good for me. If you want more, I'll be along for the ride. Happily along for the ride. If you decided you don't want more, I'll be along for that as well."

"Kat, I don't want you to give up on having children because I'm unsure."

"No, that's not how I see it." How could she say this right? "At the end of my life, I'm not going to regret not having more children, but I would regret not spending that life with you."

"That's one of the nicest things anyone has ever said to me. You are a dream come true. My dream come true."

"That's hot."

Dylan laughed and pulled Kat closer. "You haven't seen anything yet."

Kat growled then placed a kiss on the shell of Dylan's ear, then nipped it. "You are driving me crazy. Who knew a long-term talk could be such a turn on?" She trailed kisses down Dylan's neck and down to her cleavage, where her shirt was unbuttoned, then licked the hint of a breast that was peeking out from the lace edging from Dylan's bra. Kat lifted her head. "Is that all you wanted to talk about? Because I have a topic I would love to discuss." God, she hoped it was. The dinner and movie she had planned paled in comparison to where she hoped the evening was going.

"Yes, that's all I wanted to talk about." Dylan laughed, then pushed Kat back on the couch before standing and unzipping the side of her skirt and letting it fall to the floor.

Kat swallowed hard, then lay back and watched Dylan slowly, excruciatingly slow, unbutton the remaining buttons on her shirt before peeling it off her shoulders. The lace trim on her lingerie and the garter belts had Kat's heart pounding. "You are so sexy." Seriously, how did she get so lucky?

"You make me feel that way. You've always made me feel that way." Dylan climbed on the couch and straddled Kat, sliding her hands underneath Kat's shirt and bra, then cupping her breasts. "Do you have any idea how many times a day I find my mind wandering because of you? Fantasizing about you? Thinking about you taking me on this couch."

Kat moaned when Dylan squeezed her breasts, then tweaked her nipples. "Not as much as I think about you." Kat whimpered when Dylan raked her nails along the sides of her breasts and over the abs. Good grief, she was about to combust.

"I'm in charge tonight." Dylan removed her hands from under Kat's shirt to grasp her shoulders, then ground her hips against Kat. "If you talk, I stop." Dylan pushed Kat's shirt up, leaned down, and licked her abs. She stopped long enough to glance up at Kat's face. "If you understand, nod."

Kat swallowed and moaned as Dylan licked her stomach again.

"Do." Dylan squeezed Kat's breasts. "You." She moved her hands up to skim fingertips along Kat's neck, then held her head in place to look into Kat's eyes. "Understand?"

Kat nodded, then scrambled up when Dylan stood and motioned for her to follow. There was no way she was going to ruin tonight by talking. The walk to the bedroom was painfully slow, watching Dylan's shapely rear sway in front of her. A few times, she almost reached out and grabbed it, but a quick shake of Dylan's head kept her in line.

If Dylan wanted to be in charge, Kat would gladly give up control. She stood by the door, mesmerized when Dylan placed one of her legs on the bed, then turned to her and winked before unclipping her garter belt and rolling the stocking down her leg. It was the sexiest thing Kat had ever seen. She stood stock still while Dylan paid the same attention to her other leg.

Kat didn't even blink until Dylan climbed on the bed, then reclined back against the headboard, looking like the goddess she was.

"You're entirely overdressed. Take off your pants, then your shirt. Slowly. Leave your bra and underwear on. We have all night and I'm going to take my time with you."

It took all of Kat's will power not to fling her clothes off, but she went slowly, wanting Dylan to enjoy this as much as she was. Take charge Dylan was one of the most exciting things she'd ever experienced. If this was her life now, she couldn't wait to see what the future held. Being with Dylan, Kat knew, was the best decisions she'd ever made. Fate, she decided, sometimes did get it right.

Epilogue

Seven months later

Kat took a deep breath of the crisp air as she secured the rain fly onto her tent. Briley had challenged her to see who could put their tent up first, but Kat quickly realized she had the win when Briley struggled to even get her tent out of the bag. Seeing as Briley had camped with Leah and their kids a handful of times, Kat figured Briley would have learned something by now. She'd wanted to bring the camper, but Briley and Leah had quickly vetoed that idea.

"Looks like I win." Kat threw her arms up in victory and chuckled at Evan's scowl, who was only a few steps away from finishing his.

Briley glared at her but nodded in defeat. "You win; now help me put ours up."

Twenty minutes later, all four tents were up. Even though the spot for their camp wasn't Kat's first choice, it was a nice enough spot. She would have liked to be closer to the water, but understood they would have more privacy this way, considering the campsites by the lake were already crowded. Iris and Deborah were seated under the shade of a large oak tree, talking and sipping on their beers. They'd gotten to know each other well over the last few months and Kat loved seeing her mom so happy.

The rebuilding of their relationship hadn't been

easy, but all three of them had put in the time to make it work and had already broken through a few of their issues. They'd also signed up for family therapy sessions and it had done them all a world of good. Kat knew Briley was still a little wary about their mom running, but Kat had come to terms with what happened in their childhood and had chosen not to dwell on the past.

At the far end of their camp, Dylan knelt next to Emma and Griffin, looking at something Griffin was pointing to on the ground. Probably bugs, since that was what Griff was currently fascinated with. The smile on all their faces was something Kat would never take for granted. She slipped her phone out of her pocket and took a few photos.

The last seven months had flown by and even though everything wasn't smooth sailing, Kat wouldn't have had it any other way. They weren't ready for marriage, but Dylan had said yes when Kat asked her and Emma to move in with her. Emma's room was already decorated, and Kat knew, once they moved in, that she was going to lose Stripes to Emma, but she was okay with that. They'd become inseparable.

Kat waved when Dylan smiled at her, then turned to Evan, who'd called her name.

"I'm hungry." Evan twirled the tongs in his hand. "Briley said we had to wait until you fired up the grill, grill master."

Even though her relationship with Evan had always been good, after Christmas when they'd both decided to watch their family videos together, they'd grown closer. He was growing into a fine man and Kat couldn't wait to see what the future held for him. He had asked his girlfriend to join them, but her family already had plans. It was a privilege seeing him taking on more responsibility. The beard he'd grown over the last few months was filling out, but made him look so much older.

"All right. All right," Kat said and rolled her eyes.

Off to the side, Briley and Leah stood, arms around each other. Kat finally knew what that felt like. The all-consuming love that took hold of you and never let go. Their wedding was less than a month away and everyone decided that a family camping trip was the distraction they needed before their big day. With Madison almost nine months pregnant, they hadn't been able to make it, but everyone had agreed on another family camping trip when the baby was old enough to travel.

Kat fired up the grill and sorted through the cooler Briley had expertly packed. Briley may not be a pro at putting tents up, but she was a wizard when it came to organizing their food.

Emma had already claimed the following morning for fishing and Kat couldn't wait to fry up the fish they were sure to catch. She dug out the burgers Leah had pre-formed, the hotdogs Evan wanted, and the asparagus Dylan insisted on. Everything was seasoned before putting them on the grill. She looked up when Evan ran away and scooped a laughing Griffin up and tossed her in the air. She was getting so big he wouldn't be able to do that much longer.

Her eyes strayed to Dylan when she stood, patted Evan on the arm then headed in Kat's direction. Kat decided after seeing Dylan dress that morning that her body was made to wear cargo shorts. If they weren't sharing a tent with Emma, Kat would most definitely ravish Dylan.

"Earth to Kat."

Kat blinked. "Sorry."

"They're camping clothes." Dylan slipped behind her, wrapped her arms around Kat's waist, and kissed her neck.

"Well, you look fabulous in them." Kat flipped the asparagus. "You look good in anything."

"Flatterer."

Kat wrapped her free arm around Dylan. This is what she always wanted, but not something she ever thought she would have. At least not to this extent. She loved Dylan and Emma with everything she was and would do everything in her power to make sure they always knew that.

"You're thinking too hard." Kat turned, and Dylan slid in front of her, leaning into her chest. Dylan smoothed her fingers along Kat's forehead. "Nothing warrants that much thought."

"I disagree." She kissed Dylan on the temple. "We do." Kat slipped her arm around Dylan's back and underneath her shirt. "I love you."

"I love you too." Dylan pulled Kat down by her neck and kissed her.

"Are you trying to drive me crazy?" She kept her arm around Dylan as she flipped the burgers and hotdogs.

"It doesn't take much, especially when I run my tongue over that dip in your abs."

"Really now," Briley spoke up from behind them. "This is a family space. Sex talk in private."

Kat groaned and flipped Briley off. "Get the fixings out; these are almost done."

"Yes, your highness."

Leah must have heard, because she laughed, walked over, and dragged Briley off to set up the picnic table.

Five minutes later, Kat scooped everything off the grill and onto the platter, then shut the lid and gave Dylan her undivided attention. "Next camping trip, we're bringing the camper."

"Now, darling, this is an ideal bonding experience for all of us."

"If you say so. Let's be thankful we don't have to share a tent with Briley and Leah."

"I heard that," Briley shouted.

Kat wrapped her arms around her love and buried her head into the soft neck, taking a minute to nuzzle it. She nipped Dylan's ear lobe, then looked into her eyes. "I love being here with you."

"I love it too. I have something for you. Follow me." Dylan lead Kat toward their tent where their bags were. "Wait here." Dylan crawled into the tent.

"I'm not going anywhere." Kat pushed her hands in the back pocket of her jeans until Dylan crawled out of the tent. Kat gave her a hand up, then her eyes latched onto the rose in Dylan's hand.

"This is for you."

Kat took the rose and brought it up to her nose. With eyes closed, and a sniff, she smiled at the scent. "I thought I was the flower giver."

"Not this time." Dylan laid her hands on Kat's collar bones. "Its official name is Lasting Love."

"Lasting Love."

"You like the sound of that?"

"I love the sound." She rested their foreheads together. "So, you're saying you fell into lasting love with me?"

Dylan cupped her cheeks, her expression serious. "I did." She traced Kat's eyebrow with a fingertip. "I fell into a lot of things with you, darling. I never thought I'd be here, at this point in my life again. You changed everything, and I let you. My world was so empty and then, here you came."

"I wanted someone to share my life with and there you were. I knew I could give you everything you needed if you would let me." Kat searched her eyes.

"Falling with you feels like home."

Kat tangled their fingers together, pulled Dylan flush against her with her free hand, and swayed to the music only they could hear. "Do you know what falling with you feels like to me?"

"Enlighten me."

"It feels like my purpose. To love you. To love Emma. I've always questioned why things happened when I should have been asking who. Who is going to sweep me off my feet? Who is going to love me unconditionally? Who am I going to give my heart to, and will she cherish it as much as I cherish hers? Who is no longer a question that I'm asking because I know the who."

"You always say the right things."

"You know that's not true."

"It's true enough."

"So, is this thing we've got going on enough for you to keep falling with me?"

"You better believe it."

Kat kissed the back of Dylan's hand. "I don't want to ruin our moment, but your dimples are about the hottest thing I've ever seen." Kat groaned when Dylan's smile widened, and her dimples were out in full force. Kat pushed Dylan away then twirled her and brought her back.

"There's no music," Dylan whispered.

"Of course there is. Just because no one else can hear it doesn't mean it's not playing."

"A soundless song?"

"Our song. The sound of our heartbeats," Kat dipped her, then slowly brought her back up until their lips were almost touching, "The sound we can dance to anywhere."

"It sounds magical."

Kat immersed into the twinkling eyes of the woman she loved. "No, it sounds like a fairy tale come true."

About the Author

Born near Chicago, but raised in Southern Illinois, where she still lives, Shannon spends her free time writing. When she isn't writing, she enjoys binge watching fantasy, science fiction, or true crime shows.

You can contact Shannon at -

Website: smhfiction.com
Email: smh1981@live.com
Facebook: facebook.com/smharrisauthor
Twitter: @smhfiction

Check out Shannon's other books.

The Adearian Chronicles - Book One - The Oath – ISBN – 978-1-943353-17-0

Ex-mercenary, Lanis Welsh, is finally at a place in her life where she is content with what and who she is; High Priestess Anya's Protector and Lover. After an unexpected request, she has no choice but to leave Anya's protection in the hands of someone else and travel back to the one place that holds nothing but bad memories. When she is manipulated into signing an oath she has no desire to fulfill, she questions the very truths she has built her life on. As strangers become friends and enemies become allies, Lanis must face the demons from her past. It doesn't take her long to realize there is more going on than anyone could have ever foreseen and nothing and no one can be trusted.

Adearian Chronicles - Book 2 – Revelations – ISBN - 978-1-943353-33-0

What would you do if you were faced with finding and saving the one person who held your heart, but you only had two weeks to do it?

When the unexpected happens and Lanis's world is turned upside down, she and Elson have no choice but to align themselves with two people from a strange land. With new enemies at play, and a Goddess that seems to have forsaken them, Lanis relies on the only people she can; her friends. To fight the demons that plague her daily, she has to separate her love for Anya, from the task she must perform. On top of the unknowns, she is gifted with a small black book that changes the way she sees everything and everyone around her. As her world starts to crumble, Lanis must face her fears and the nightmares that invade her dreams. With the hours ticking away, she must come to terms with the fact that she might already be too late.

The DragonWitch Tales: An Unexpected Beginning – ISBN – 978-1-943353-43-9

Death ignited her powers. Love binds them.

Paisley's normal, boring life is shattered one evening when a strange, but sexy woman appears out of thin air in her living room and claims Paisley as her wife. Things spiral out of control when Paisley is informed by her mother that she is a witch that comes from a long line of witches, that other realms exist, and that the strange woman really is her wife.

As her choices slip from her grasp, Paisley must learn to navigate her new life, a new world, and a new wife. As if that wasn't enough, Paisley must deal with a growing attraction for a new woman in her life. Throw in a dragon egg, an angry queen, a traitor, and Paisley realizes she's going to have to learn to watch every move she makes.

As the push and pull between two women and her powers reach a standoff, Paisley makes a choice that will change the course of her life and the future of the world she calls home even if that means destroying her own happiness in the process.

The Details in the Design – ISBN – 978-1-943353-79-8

Every stitch tells a story.

Avery Michaels has longed to work in the fashion industry since she was six years old. Now at thirty-two she's fed up with her job as a food critic and signs up with an employment agency that promises to find anyone their dream job.

She is thrilled when she gets an interview with the fashion house of her choice, Catherine Davenport Designs. There's only one problem. For the past six years, Avery has had a massive crush on Catherine, one of the hottest fashion designers of the past two decades.

In the midst of a new job, nosey friends, Catherine's meddling daughters, difficult co-workers, and a dachshund named Polly, Avery also has to contend with a new woman that enters Catherine's life.

From the start, Avery knows winning Catherine's heart will be no easy feat. When curve ball after curve ball is thrown her way, does she scrap her design or make it work?

Add Romance and Mix – ISBN – 978-1-948232-06-7

Briley Anderson hasn't been in a serious relationship for the past two years. The pain of her last breakup has made her weary of giving her heart away again. She spends her days flipping houses and her down-time baking treats for her neighbors. Falling in love wasn't in her plans, but then again, neither was her next-door neighbor.

Leah Daniels is a divorced mother of two and a grandmother at the age of forty-nine. Love was the last thing she was looking for, especially with a woman sixteen years her junior. All she was hoping for was a quiet neighborhood to raise her fifteen-year old son. What she hadn't expected was the unavoidable draw she felt toward Briley.

Through laughter, heartache, love, and fear it's up to Briley and Leah to figure out if what they've created is strong enough to make a relationship last and if taking the chance on love is really worth the risk.

Other books by Sapphire Authors

Highland Dew – ISBN – 978-1-948232-11-1

Bryce Andrews, west coast sales director for Global Distillers and Distribution, is tired of the corporate hamster wheel. She needs a change.

A craft whisky trade show offers her inspiration and a chance to revisit Scotland and the majestic scenery of the Speyside region—best known for the "Whisky Trail." Bryce and her coworker, Reggie Ballard, need to find a wholly original whisky for their international distribution division by visiting a number of small distillers.

A blind curve, a dangling sign, and weed-choked driveway draw Bryce directly into a truly unique opportunity. She discovers a struggling family, a shuttered distillery, and a spitfire of a daughter called home to care for her confused father.

Fiona McDougall—the only child and heir to the MacDougall & Son legacy, had her career teaching in Edinburgh curtailed by fate…or serendipity.

When the stars finally align, the two women work together to resurrect a dream for themselves and the family business—if they can weather the storms of unscrupulous business practices in the competitive whisky market.

McCall - ISBN - 978-1-948232-32-6

Sara Brighton is a quickly rising culinary star in Savannah after Food & Wine magazine named her restaurant Best New Restaurant of the South, until it burns to the ground in an accident and she impulsively packs her truck and heads for McCall, Idaho, the last place she remembers being truly happy.

Sam Draper, head of the Lake Patrol division of the McCall PD, knows the last thing she needs is another entitled tourist making her life difficult on the water. However, after Sara surprises her by helping her avoid a near professional disaster, Sam teaches her to drive a boat. The chemistry between them is hot and instant, and as the summer heats up, Sam finds herself falling in love until Sara buys her late father's iconic diner and turns it into the newest hotspot for pretentious culinary tourists.

Can the love Sam and Sara found on the water survive the lingering ghosts waiting for them back on dry land?

Silver Love – ISBN – 978-1-948232-51-7

Jill, Dory, Robby, and Charlene are a fantastic foursome that embodies the varying experiences that come with being Lesbians of a Certain Age. They are vibrant and vulnerable, wise and foolish, introspective and outgoing. The close-knit friends fight aging at every turn—or just ignore it altogether. These four will never go quietly into the night, redefining life after fifty. They are the new mature woman.

But along with twenty-first-century attitudes come twenty-first-century problems. Public office candidate and retired judge Charlene is confronted by a wannabe blackmailer, Jill's passions threaten to swamp her common sense, Dory's best-selling book could turn out to be a national disaster, and Robby must confront the hard reality of learning that her wife may not be the woman she thought she was. Steadfast in their faith in themselves and each other, and bolstered by the rich history of their friendship, the four women struggle with twists and turns as they try to navigate a landscape generated by the actions of others as well as their own choices, proving that experience does not always pave a smooth road.

In a world where everything increasingly seems relative, these women remind us that some things don't change—like the bedrock of relationships. Silver Love is all about love; love among friends, love between lovers, and the unexpected role of love with acquaintances who may not always be what they seem.

If you can keep up, join the ride and follow these ageless heroines as they pursue their adventures in the modern world.

Twisted Deception - ISBN - 978-1-939062-47-5

There are two types of people who can't look you in the eyes: someone trying to hide a lie and someone trying to hide their love.

Addie Blake's life isn't black and white—more like a series of short bursts of color that sustain her until the next eruption. She isn't a ladder-climber in the corporate world. Instead, she works long hours at the office and even at home, something her mechanic girlfriend, Drake Hogan, can't stand. If Addie can't focus on Drake, then Drake finds arm candy that will. After a long week of late nights and a series of text-messaged demands, each one a bigger bomb than the last, Addie has had enough of her Motor Girl.

Greyson Hollister inhabits a world where everything is either black and white, or money green. She's a polished, certified workaholic. As head of Integrated Financial, she has built the ladder others want to climb. Now she intends to attend a business mixer to confront a rumormonger and kill merger rumors involving her company.

Detective Nancy Hill, the lead detective on the Elevator Rapist task force, has just been called in to investigate an attack at Integrated Financial. She can't quite put her finger on it, but something doesn't add up with this latest assault, and Greyson Hollister isn't exactly lending a helping hand.

A storm's brewing on the horizon. Can Addie and Greyson weather it, or will it blow them over?

Bobbi and Soul *– ISBN – 978-1-948232-41-8*

Bobbi Webster wants nothing more than to be the best family practice doctor for her home town in rural Oregon. To accomplish that, she's enrolled in a two-year fellowship in rural medicine at Valley View Medical Center in Colorado. Sparks fly when Bobbi meets the Reverend Erin O'Rouke, a petite, feisty priest who meddles in the treatment of Bobbi's patients. To make matters worse, Bobbi wants nothing to do with any religion, much less the woman she dubs, The Elf.

Erin serves as vicar at a small church where a few parishioners have stipulated that she must be celibate, reflecting their "love the sinner, hate the sin" tactic. After she clashes with Erin, Bobbi recognizes how a recent breakup of an abusive relationship has falsely colored her perception of Erin's world and work. Likewise, when Erin understands how Bobbi's emotional wounds make her vulnerable, her natural empathy moves her closer to Bobbi.

They find themselves drawn to each other, but how can Bobbi and Erin overcome so many obstacles to find love?

Hearts INN – ISBN – 978-1-948232-36-4

Rosalie Campbell is bequeathed a rundown hotel in rural New Mexico in her grandmother's will. She arrives to discover a dried-out shell of a place that barely makes enough money to stay afloat. In a state of limbo with her girlfriend and accounting job in Philadelphia, Rosalie is keen to sell the hotel and go back to the comfort of her urban life. When new information about her grandmother surfaces and the hotel proves difficult to sell, Rosalie tries to attract buyers by restoring the building to its former glory with the help of Alex Ecker, a local handywoman. In the process, Rosalie learns a few things about hotel management, hard work, and opening her heart.

www.ingramcontent.com/pod-product-compliance
Lightning Source LLC
Chambersburg PA
CBHW030107100526
44591CB00009B/310